MARY KEY, Ph.D.

Seizing
Success

A WOMAN'S GUIDE TO TRANSFORMAT

D1115153

"In Seizing Success, *Mary Key* has combined her substantial theoretical and conceptual knowledge with her extensive coaching and teaching experience to create strategies to become a great leader. She applies these for women through the lens of being a woman."

— **JOSEPH HOPKINS, MD**, Clinical Professor of Medicine, Director of the Stanford University Leadership Development Program for Healthcare

"Women struggle with feeling the pressure to perform. Mary Key aces it in identifying why women often recoil from pressure and what to do about it. The strategies offered in Seizing Success *serve as a guidepost for women at any stage of their careers, especially those starting out."*

— **DR. HENDRIE WEISINGER**, Author of New York Times Best Selling Book, *Performing under Pressure*

"You can customize your new car, a pair of jeans and an omelet. Why would you not customize your career, or better yet, your life? Mary Key, in her brilliant, engaging new book, will help you do just that. You'll get clear about what you really want... and you'll discover strategies and steps for how to get it. Every woman who aspires to lead others should read Seizing Success!"

— **SHARON JORDAN-EVANS**, co-author of the Best-seller *Love 'Em or Lose 'Em: Getting Good People to Stay."*

"I heard Mary Key speak to an organization of professional women that I belong to and she was terrific! Many of the stories and strategies she spoke about are in this book. I was impressed by her understanding of leadership and her ability to break it down in relatable, practical advice."

— **LORNA TAYLOR**, President & CEO, Premier Eye Care

"Real change happens when groups of men and women begin practicing, and not just talking about, new behaviors in the workplace. Seizing Success *is an extraordinary guide to the practices women can cultivate and men can respect and respond to at work. Drawn from her extensive coaching experiences and women's leadership groups, Mary offers down to earth tools and inspiring strategies for achieving uncompromising excellence at work and a balanced life worth living."*

— **ALAN BRISKIN**, Author, *The Stirring of Soul in the Workplace* and *The Power of Collective Wisdom*

"Over 40 years of experience in the leadership space and working with executives and leaders primarily in Fortune 100 companies has provided me with insights as to the importance of one's personal compass. In particular, the relevance not only of identifying one's personal values, but implementing them in our personal and professional lives. Seizing Success: A Woman's Guide to Transformational Leadership provides the much needed and essential strategies for implementing one's personal values, which, in turn, energizes everything. The crucial relevance of a personal and professional compass enables us to live a purposeful and dynamic existence. This book will not only be read and handy on my nightstand, but will be required reading for women I coach, lead, and mentor."

— **CECELIA K. HOUSER, Ed.D**., Principal, Korn Ferry

"For women at all stages of their careers, building trusted relationships is just one of the many keys to transforming leadership that Mary explores in her book, and one that's critical for advancing women to corporate boards. A must-read for any woman serious about leading."

— **BETSY BERKHEMER-CREDAIRE**, CEO of 2020 Women on Boards and author of *The Board Game: How Smart Women Become Corporate Directors*

"Mary has been in the perfect position to learn the issues that face women leaders. Not only has she "been there" and "done that" herself, but she has coached countless women in facing and overcoming them. Mary brings her years of experience to women in every stage in their careers. Bravo."

— **Dr. BEVERLY KAYE**, Co-author, Love 'Em or Lose 'Em, *Help Them Grow or Watch Them Go* and *Up is Not the Only Way*

"Winning in business and being successful in the competitive environment is all about leadership, teamwork, and focus. Dr. Key offers strategies, tools and insights into how it's done and what's really important."

— **ANGEL RUIZ**, President & CEO, Ericsson North America

To women everywhere
who are willing to take the lead
for themselves and for others.

Your Visual Map
to Navigating this Book

Inside Yourself
- Confidence
- Right Focus
- Pressure to Perform

You & Others
- Assertivness
- Influence

You in the World
- Transformational Leadership
- Power of Peers

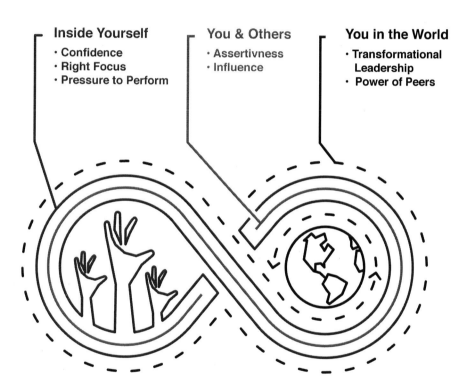

Table of
Contents

Seizing Success

A WOMEN'S GUIDE TO TRANSFORMATIONAL LEADERSHIP

Introduction

Make no mistake. Our time is now. The opportunities are opening. The environment has changed. The time is ripe for you. Look around you—at politics, culture, maybe even your own office—and you'll see how much things have changed. The renewed focus on equal pay, more equality in the workplace, and expanded leadership roles are the result of very real economic, social, legal and political pressure brought to bear by the raised voices of women. If there's a moment's doubt about that power, take a look at the #metoo movement's remarkable transformative force.

You might be following an entrepreneurial path or pursuing a promotion. Or maybe you're considering a switch to a different job, even a different career path altogether, to make your work life better fit your passions, values and abilities.

A record number of women are running for public office. Politico reports that over 25 years ago after the "Year of the Woman," women only made up one in five of the elected officials in Congress. In the recent election cycle a record number of women declared their intention to run for the House, Senate or governor. Many won. Women now make up nearly a quarter of the voting membership of Congress, the most ever in US history.

The same is true in the corporate world. Initiatives like 2020 Women on Boards have taken off. 2020 Women on Boards is a national campaign to increase the percentage of women on US company boards of directors to 20% or greater by 2020. In the latest report, the percentage of women on corporate boards is now at 17.3%. Over 25 cities around the country are participating in awareness events to support getting more women on board seats. Companies are being ordered to add women executives to their boards. For example, California has become the first state to require corporate boards to include women.

I've seen firsthand the struggles women in leadership roles encounter that are different, and often more difficult from any challenges faced by men in comparable roles. I've also seen up close the unique strengths that women leaders can bring to the table when they get a seat like willingness to find common ground, collaboration and hard work. The current climate is better than ever for you to advance now and in the future.

Seizing Success: A Woman's Guide to Transformational Leadership charts a map for you to improve, enhance, refine, and further develop your leadership capabilities. It will help you hone your strategic career planning and personal goal-setting. The skill areas or competencies outlined in this book come from the needs and opportunities most frequently brought up by women in leadership roles – through women's forums that I've started and facilitated, through the executive coaching and leadership development work done over the years and through the research out there on what women in leadership can benefit from the most. Each chapter is designed to provide a clear understanding of a core competency that will strengthen and enhance your leadership capabilities and help you achieve your highest wishes for yourself and ultimately, those you lead.

The underlying principle guiding the book is the emphasis on developing and strengthening an open attitude toward aiming higher and trying new things to develop your leadership skills. Some call this a growth mindset vs. a fixed or entrenched mindset. What's the difference?

If you have a fixed mindset, you may tend to hold on to what you know and defend your status. You see having to work hard at something as an indicator that you don't have the aptitude—so you don't try. By contrast, when you have a growth mindset, you approach a given task as a perpetual learner. You view the struggle of learning something new as part of self-development, and see competence as something you can build. You see intelligence as developable and not something you are just born with. You believe that you can shape your own course in life.

A growth mindset enhances your confidence and sets the stage for you to take risks. You're willing to try new things even when you know that you won't always be successful.

Learning often involves failing temporarily. We as women are often more risk-averse than men. I've seen women hesitate and not go after a promotion or pitch an idea because they fear failure or they don't feel 100% qualified. Why?

We as women have been taught to get good grades, be nice and wait our turn. Many of us haven't been groomed to go after what we want and to learn that failure is a good thing. It's often the short-term failures that teach us most. They usually lead to long term success if we have the resilience to weather the storms.

The timing for women to lead has never been better and you are not alone. In this book, I will share true stories about the peer groups I've facilitated and how women have benefited from regularly meeting with each other to share their pictures of success and receive support and advice from other peers. Women are stronger together.

I'm the founder of the Key Women's Leadership Forum: http://keyas-sociatesinc.com/womens-leadership-forum/. The purpose of the Key Women's Leadership Forum is to bring together women in leadership roles and focus on the whole self – mind, body, spirit and career. In our monthly peer forums participants address pressing issues, improve how to leverage their influence and align their careers with what is purposeful for them. The goal is not to help women "fit in" to an established structure unless they choose to, but to provide the support and a brain trust needed to help each other grow and act.

This book can help you accelerate your career and find more joy and fulfillment in your life. You'll find clarity on your personal mission, vision and values. In doing so, you'll get in touch with a unique internal compass that can guide and support you through the opportunities and challenges in life. Your mindset may change as you open up to new ways of doing things. You will learn about strategies that will help you develop or enhance competencies that women in leadership have that makes them successful. It's time for you to seize success!

Done is better than perfect

-

Sheryl Sandberg

Chapter 1:

Confidence — The Secret Sauce

Betty runs to the bathroom and throws up. She dreads presenting to coworkers and invited guests at the quarterly company meeting. She goes on in fifteen minutes.

The last time she spoke to this group, her boss, the CEO, corrected her in front of everyone. "I think what Betty is trying to say…" was among the phrases he used to interrupt her. It was bad enough that she painstakingly planned her talk and triple-checked it for accuracy—the process of writing a 15-minute talk ate up multiple hours, and she second-guessed and doubted her judgement at every step. But to be publicly challenged that way was mortifying.

Betty lost confidence in herself. She feels that no matter what she does she will never be effective in the CEO's estimation. Once confident in her abilities, she now hesitates. She is afraid of making a mistake and continues to play back past situations in her mind, wondering if she should have done things differently.

Confidence is one of our most sought-after traits, in life and in business. Confident people accomplish what they want to get done without excessive agonizing, doubt, or rumination. An air of certainty wins others to their side—even when their work isn't perfect. Out of the hundreds of women I've worked with as a coach and peer forum facilitator, most expressed a wish for more confidence, or told a story in which their lack of it held them back. Research backs up its importance: confidence does more to build respect and influence in a group than actual competence. We've identified it as the most fundamental of the core leadership competencies in this book that will help you excel in your career and life.

So why aren't Betty and women like her more confident? It's not for lack of talent or intelligence—Betty knew her subject inside and out. It's certainly not because women don't know that confidence is an asset. Rather, a lot if it has to do with the people we're surrounded by and the environment in which we work.

The female leaders we coach and the women participating in our Key Women's Leadership Forum report that they either work in an environment like Betty's—one that saps their confidence—or they have in the past. Their stories include characters who sound similar. Such as the division leader who cares more about feeling like the smartest person in the room than helping the team get ahead. The boss who responds to smart critiques with eye rolls and statements like "those aren't the real numbers." The CEO who sees no problem with publicly embarrassing a valuable colleague. Sound familiar?

I have sat in executive team meetings and boardrooms and watched this dynamic play out countless times. Companies and careers suffer. This type of poor leadership can affect anyone, male and female—but there's another thing we notice. Women, more than men, allow external factors like an egocentric CEO or a toxic culture to chip away at their confidence.

So what's the solution? All that triple-checking and careful planning isn't getting us where we need to be. Today's female leaders need clear, targeted techniques to build confidence and bolster it when it begins to sag.

 ## What we know

When confidence depends too much on others and not on our own internal state of mind, it flounders. Even the most confident among us can fall prey to a toxic environment where we begin to second guess ourselves. Confidence is sapped by criticism, especially from people in power over us. We sometimes collude with the toxic environments we get caught up in, creating a vicious cycle that undermines our belief in ourselves.

In their book *The Confidence Code*, Claire Shipman and Katty Kay assert that the main reason women are less confident than men is because they tend to lack self-belief: Instead of simply acting, they stop to think about why they might fail. Shipman and Kay cite many studies to support their conclusion. Even successful women who have obviously made it in their careers are more likely to hesitate before acting or initiating than men.

I had a chance to reflect on this dynamic when I was invited to speak at Raymond James' Women in Capital Markets Conference. I was excited to hear that Claire Shipman was the keynote speaker. In her talk, Shipman recounted interviews she and Kay conducted with some of the most powerful women in the world, one of whom was über-attorney Christine Lagarde, managing director of the International Monetary Fund.

Lagarde admitted that she worries about getting caught off-guard in her many business interactions, and at times has to dig deep to gain her confidence to assert a particular point. Her way of addressing this momentary lapse in confidence is to over-prepare. She focuses on avoiding any possible error or misunderstanding for which she could be criticized. Even more interesting, Lagarde found that her friend Angela Merkel, the German chancellor and another of the world's most powerful women, does the same thing. Both women developed the same habit of scrutinizing every aspect of work in order to, in Lagarde's words, "Be completely on top of everything." She confessed, "It's very time-consuming!"

In my leadership development work, I've had the privilege to talk with many women in positions of power. What I learned is that many of them feel this same overwhelming fear of making a mistake. The fear often takes the form of overanalyzing a situation. Instead of acting on what they believe or know, women tend to second-guess themselves—even if their knowledge and instincts prove right time and time again.

Hours spent rewriting a speech for the fifth time, or crafting the perfect response to a casual email from the boss are hours not spent on strategic priorities. Productivity and effectiveness suffer. Women who over-analyze pay a price. They may be successful, but not necessarily happy because they allow their internal state to be in constant anticipation of what must be "fixed" so they don't get caught off-guard.

So why do we do these things? Perhaps it's because as little girls, we learn to be "good" and earn rewards for being perfect. Some of us get addicted to pleasing others. A vast body of research suggests that women tend to see the risks in a situation and hold back, while for men it's "act now, think later" (Campbell). This gender difference in behavior is particularly salient in the workplace because it increases under stress (Mather and Lightall). It's very pronounced in situations where a person stands to lose or gain money—another key feature of workplace decisions.

In 2012, a team of economists conducted a meta-analysis on experiments from all over the world in which subjects were asked to play an investment game; the studies consistently found that women invest less and are more wary of financial risk (Charness and Gneezy). Whether investing your own funds or trying to make the best use of your company's assets, taking the right risk can yield big rewards. Perfectionism can stand in the way of success.

Another factor which erodes confidence is the inability for some to see their accomplishments clearly. Many people—especially women—suffer from imposter syndrome, the feeling of inadequacy and self-doubt in spite of a track record of success and displaying competence. Women may feel like frauds and attribute their successes to external factors like luck, being liked, or working harder than others. "Imposters" have difficulty internalizing their accomplishment. Despite their often-significant achievements, the fear of being discovered haunts them. They wrongly adopt the premise that since their accomplishments aren't based on competence, they will be found out. Instead of enjoying attaining goals or promotions, the imposter waits anxiously for others to discover that she doesn't deserve them.

Some researchers have linked the imposter syndrome with perfectionism (Dudau; Vergauwe *et al.*). With imposter syndrome, a cycle of achievement triggers a fear of failure. Fear ignites perfectionistic behavior that can take the form of over-preparing, downplaying progress, or procrastinating. When a task is accomplished or a goal reached, the "imposter" begins to discount achievement, setting up a cycle of ongoing anxiety and lack of fulfillment.

We could use new framing

Developing and building confidence involves overcoming our own fears. For some, confidence levels can be temporarily impacted based on a situation. For others, feeling confident can be a constant challenge. Confidence requires courage, operating more from our heart than our head, a willingness to pursue our dreams, and stepping forward for a cause and/or a willingness to lead others. Confidence requires self-awareness, an intention to purge perfection, and the willingness to take calculated risks for the right reasons.

If, like Betty, you work in a toxic culture where you fear making a mistake or are questioned by people in authority, your confidence can crumble. Leading with confidence involves overcoming your own fears—facing situations without being overwhelmed or knocked off course by external factors. Today's workplace requires courageous leadership.

The word "courage" comes from the French *coeur*, meaning heart. Leading courageously gives "heart" or encouragement to others—the courage to pursue your dreams, to lead others, to be the very best *you*, you can be. This kind of leadership has a trickle-down effect on an organization and contributes to its success.

It's difficult to act courageously in some organizations, even when you are the CEO or part of the leadership team. The culture can get away from you when you don't pay close attention or fear reprisal. What gets modeled and rewarded is what gets done. If others in leadership roles are behaving badly or accepting bad behavior, it sends a message.

Betty thought that over-preparing and obsessively checking her work for errors was what she needed to do because it dampened her anxiety for a while. In reality, this approach wasted her time, and when her boss spotted an error she felt worse than ever. What feels right in the moment can take you down the wrong path. In the heat of your uneasiness, you may develop a habit or pattern of behavior that doesn't help you in the long run. These patterns become ingrained and you may fall back on them automatically, creating a ferocious cycle. (After all, the more you tell yourself that your big presentation has to be flawless, the more dread and fear you experience.)

How aware are you of the patterns that deplete your confidence? Those that build it? Where are the pivot points for you? Becoming aware of your behavior and how it impacts others is the first step toward change. In Betty's case, she didn't realize that her fearful response and perfectionistic behavior impacted her team. When she asked them for honest feedback on how the team was doing, one of them said "I feel like we're focusing on problems more than on the important things, like setting goals together and achieving them. I'm tired of walking on eggshells." They felt as if Betty's focus on pleasing someone they didn't even respect—her hyper-critical supervisor—caused her to lose sight of the team's true goals and needs.

One of the keys to building confidence is the very thing people who lack confidence try to avoid—mistakes and failure. You learn from taking risks, including those that don't work out. Challenging experiences help to nurture your competence and seed confidence. Experiencing failure from an early age can forge a lifelong habit of resilience. Women who learn from failure instead of recoiling from it see it as a lesson they can apply in the future. They realize that they can bounce back from setbacks and mistakes, which fosters the courage to act.

The Marines have a policy they call "bias for action"—a preference for doing something rather than nothing, even when the information about possible outcomes is imperfect. The rationale is that by acting promptly on the available information, you're more responsive to changing circumstances. Getting all the information about a given situation is not possible. If you hold out for 100 percent accuracy, analysis paralysis may occur, something that's dangerous in life-threatening situations. Imagine a military unit that receives conflicting information about the location of the enemy. If commanders make a decision about which report is more reliable they may strike first. If they wait to be certain, they're sitting ducks. "Bias for action" was put in place to encourage decision-makers to gather facts and formulate a strategy—quickly. Women in leadership can learn a lot from this approach. Whether you dash off an email, make a new hire, or sign off on a multimillion-dollar ad campaign, be as thorough as you can, but act!

Another contributor to building confidence is developing a growth mindset. In her book *Mindset: The New Psychology of Success*, researcher Dr. Carol Dweck outlines the distinction between a "fixed" and a "growth" mindset. In the first, you view your amount of intelligence and talent as limited and unlikely to change over time. In the second type of mindset, you view yourself as going through a process of learning and self-development and see competency as something you can build.

People with a fixed mindset tend to defend their status and hold on to what they know. They may work hard to prevent mistakes while avoiding putting in the effort to learn new things. To them, having to work hard at something means that they don't have the aptitude. By contrast, people with a growth mindset are willing to try new things, even if they initially fail. They set performance goals and work on ways to achieve them. They don't think of mistakes as reflecting on their intelligence, because intelligence is something they continuously develop. People with growth mindsets believe that they can shape their own course in life. Which best describes you?

5 Strategies to Seize Success While Enhancing Confidence

Here are five effective strategies to build or enhance your confidence. As you read, see if one or several appeal to you as an approach with which you can experiment.

Action A: Purge perfectionism

Perfectionism is sometimes justified as having high standards. No one brags about low standards. You go too far when you become consumed with "getting everything right" and lose your sense of priorities. Think about your most challenging current project, and what it would take for you to be happy with your work on it. Are your standards realistic? Are you disappointed in yourself because you don't feel like you're achieving all you had hoped? Are you fearful that what you can deliver isn't good enough? Are other areas of your life suffering as a result?

If so, you may have crossed the line from having high standards to perfectionism. Possessing perfectionist tendencies puts you at risk for developing mental health issues ranging from eating disorders, substance abuse, and chronic stress, to workaholism and depression.

In their book *Just Enough*, Harvard professors Laura Nash and Howard Stevenson researched high-achieving professionals, including attendees of Harvard executive programs and members of the Young Presidents Organization. Although they did not focus on perfectionism specifically, their findings offer important takeaways for anyone who demands a lot from themselves. High achievers can cross the line into perfectionism which robs them of true happiness. They become so focused on one big professional goal that friendships, family, and health suffer. The antidote that the authors offer is to look at success and identify what it means to you in relation to four components: happiness, achievement, significance, and legacy. Instead of trying to excel in all of these areas, or only in the achievement arena, identify what is "just enough" for you in each category. Balance is the key.

Set a plan that energizes you, not one that deflates you. Stop comparing yourself to others; force yourself to be adequate in some areas so you have time to excel in the important stuff. For example, you may have a big goal in the achievement area such as being the successor to the CEO. If that's your top priority you may not be able to learn Mandarin…and be on the board of a charity…and do triathlons on the weekends. Instead of setting such high expectations in all areas of your life, find what's comfortable. Decide to run 5 miles 3 times a week instead of also setting the goal of competing in a triathlon. As the authors point out, high achievers who find a balance in the goals they set report being happier.

Action B: Take risks and act

Successful leaders take calculated risks. The next time you consider different options such as "Should I ask for a pay raise this quarter?" or "Should my team focus resources on our new product instead of growing our established one?", start by conducting a simple risk analysis. First, explore your answers to the following questions: "What is the best thing that can happen if I take this risk and act?" and "Is the benefit worth the risk?" Next, ask yourself, "What's the worst thing that can happen if I take this course of action?" "Can I live with the consequences?"

If the benefits outweigh the risks and you can live with the consequences, go forward with confidence. Reframe your thinking from viewing risk as a negative to viewing your bold stance or move as a challenge—one that you can grow from no matter what, even at first if you don't succeed.

One of our Key Women's Leadership Forum participants, we'll call her Jennifer, was offered a new position as vice president of marketing for a consumer products company. Although her current position had the same title, the new opportunity offered more responsibility in terms of number of staff, size of budget, and scope of work. Jennifer was excited but hesitant because she wasn't sure she was "ready" for such a "big job." As we went through the process of best- and worst-case analysis, she realized that if she had the chance to expand into this role and failed, she could live with her choice more easily than if she took the safe route and remained in a stagnant position.

 # Action C: Act "as if" and let go

The latest research in neuroscience and physiology indicates that our expressions, gestures, and body positioning impact how we feel.

Studies on the animal kingdom as well as with humans show that our body language and gestures make a difference in our emotional state and in the reaction of others (Lillie; Wlassoff).

Smile and you start feeling happier. Your body chemistry changes for the better and influences how you feel. Strike a powerful pose like the universal victory stance (hands up in a V, legs comfortably apart while standing tall) and hold it for several minutes—in private, of course. You prime yourself to enter a high-stakes meeting feeling like a winner. Position yourself by sitting and standing up straight and using body movements that fill space and you will feel more like a leader. Act "as if" you are where you deserve to be or have achieved what you want to do. As social psychologist Amy Cuddy writes in her book *Presence*, the right stance helps you face high-stakes moments "with confidence and excitement instead of doubt and dread" (18).

What about fear? Similar to most people's discomfort discussing money and death, I notice that many people in business are reluctant to talk about fear. Yet fear of not performing well or failing is more common than people think. In one of our peer forums where 8 to 10 CEOs come together regularly to discuss business and leadership issues, a CEO blurted out, "I get up in the middle of the night and can't go back to sleep." "What's wrong?" asked one of the other participants. The CEO took a deep breath and responded: "I have fear—fear that things won't work out, fear that my business will not succeed, and fear of what I don't know."

Most of the others chimed in with similar experiences. The CEOs trust each other because the group has met for almost two years. An energetic and honest conversation ensued. It was clear that leaders feel the pressure to make decisions, take calculated risks, and do the right thing for those who depend on them.

The real choice is to let go. How do you get past strong emotions so you can choose your attitude? Psychiatrist, consciousness researcher, and philosopher Dr. David Hawkins wrote in his book *Letting Go* about a process for controlling emotions that really works:

1. Be aware of the feeling and let it come up.

2. Allow yourself to experience the feeling without resisting it; suspend any tendency to judge, fear, or moralize about it. No self-talk, just feel the emotion.

3. Stay with the feeling and let it run its course without trying to change anything. Ignore your thoughts and focus totally on the feeling itself. It will dissipate.

Acting "as if" is easier when you can let go or mitigate fear. Try acting "as if" in combination with letting go for powerful results.

Remember Betty, the nervous public speaker we discussed at the beginning of the chapter? Every time she sat down to work on her presentation she felt a stress response including an elevated heartbeat and a desire to escape the task. She reacted with self-talk—telling herself she made lots of mistakes on her last presentation and she had to work even harder on this one. Her stress levels remained high throughout each session as she criticized every line she wrote. Instead, imagine if she used the letting go technique. She sits quietly for a few moments, observes her racing heart, takes some deep breaths, and lets her pulse start to slow. She reminds herself that her stress response is just a passing emotion, not a reflection of her competence or ability to complete the presentation.

With her new, calmer frame of mind, she can set some realistic goals for the session, such as "write a draft of the section on customer retention and ask one trusted ally for feedback." Instead of letting anxiety compel her to keep working until she is exhausted, she can move on to the next task and pick up work the next day.

Remaining calm and meeting her goals during her preparation sessions, Betty can walk in on presentation day nervous but in control. She can make a point to stand with her shoulders back and head high, knowing the speech will be a hit. Her boss might still criticize her, but she will feel content with her work and connect more easily with others in the audience who are receptive to her message.

Action D: Cultivate a growth mindset

The concept of cultivating a growth mind set is based on the principle that you can develop capabilities, skills, and abilities with which you weren't born. It's about taking an active role in creating your own future and seeing new challenges as a learning experience. Research shows that people who are presented with new tasks in a performance situation are more risk averse and less likely to experiment or innovate than those who are presented with the tasks in a learning situation. (Edmondson). When you are in a learning mode, it's ok to experiment and make mistakes. Remind yourself that making mistakes can be a good thing. See your environment as a learning experience or your own personal growth workshop.

You might consider:

- Viewing a challenge as an opportunity – ask, what can I learn from this?
- Expanding your options to address the challenge
- Seeing the value of the process for your growth vs. just the outcome
- Connecting your actions to a larger sense of purpose or direction
- Rewarding yourself for making progress, even when you have struggled

Action E: Use the power of intention

When you feel bombarded with challenges and competing demands, taking time to adopt a learning orientation may be the last thing on your mind. Putting out whatever fire is doing the most damage seems crucial, and making long-term plans or learning a new way can wait, right? One of the women in our forum, "Alice," went into business for herself a few years ago as a digital marketing consultant. She reported in her update that she felt caught in a maze of to-do lists, eating on the run, and responding to texts and emails from her kids, vendors, and customers from morning till late at night. She felt trapped. If a potential customer asked a question, she felt pressure to respond right away so they wouldn't lose interest. If a client complained, she offered apologies and discounts so as to keep their business—even if the work they wanted done wasn't what she dreamed of doing. Isn't the customer (or boss, or investor, or…fill in the blank) always right?

If you stay in a reactive mode, you continually react to other people's needs, always working on what someone else thinks is most important. Start from the inside and set your intention. Intentionality breeds confidence. In his many inspiring books, motivational psychologist Dr. Wayne Dyer writes about intention and how getting in touch with your intention can change your life from a fear-based existence to an empowered one. Dyer points out that many people stay miserable because they see themselves as alone and fear the future.

In *The Power of Intention*, Dyer describes intention as an ever-present and infinite energy source that we can all tap into consciously. A prerequisite for setting and acting on your intention is accepting that a higher energy source exists: what some call God or the Universe. By developing self-awareness, you can state your intentions through positive affirmations and visualization, resulting in a shift in your way of thinking and being. For example, affirming that "I am confident and competent in all I do" sets the intention and repeating this affirmation helps reshape any negative self-talk that chips away at your confidence. Picturing yourself confident and competent enhances the outcome.

Dyer's advice on how to co-create a more confident world is to tap into this higher energy source and examine what is most purposeful for you. As affirmations and visualizations become reality, confidence blossoms. A strong connection to a higher source gives you strength beyond yourself; you aren't doing it alone, but by accessing a higher power that anyone can call upon.

Commitment is easier when you have clarity and have weighed your alternatives. Once you do that, you need resilience. You have to return to your goal even when you feel discouraged or have had a setback.

Seizing Success: Brooke's Story

Brooke left the world of big accounting firms to start a financial services business that provides CFO services to companies. She and her team brought a unique style of financial competence with a "refreshingly human" customer service approach. Her company grew from working mostly in-state to multiple states. She constantly hired new team members. As her company grew larger, so did the challenges. It became harder to retain key staff; most reported they felt burnt out. Brooke started to feel the same way and began to lose confidence in her ability to lead the company. She began entertaining offers to sell her company. The advice she received from her forum group was to take a personal retreat, make time for herself, and think through the options.

As Brooke took time to relax, she tried not to think about the business. She used the time away to meditate and focus on staying in the present moment. As her retreat came to a close, she set her intentions for herself and how she pictured the business to be. Refreshed, Brooke re-committed to her goal of building a unique company. She re-evaluated the structure and brainstormed ways she could re-balance the work for herself and the team.

Upon her return, Brooke felt more confident in her commitment to build the company and bring its unique mission to her clients. She held an off-site meeting to get her team's input. Together they brainstormed some ways to streamline and better balance the distribution of work tasks, and cut some services that weren't contributing to client and company growth. Each member of the team clarified their intention in going forward. The group was able to support the growth of the business without experiencing the same levels of stress. Their support for each other and confidence in their next steps grew.

Making a commitment requires aligning, not just your thoughts, but also your feelings and behavior with the direction you have selected. Commitment is the sum total of the behaviors you display that either supports your intention or detracts from it.

 ## Review the five growth strategies in this chapter

You have now read about five actionable strategies that can improve and enhance your self-confidence and more. Select those that attract you and experiment. These are:

     A. Purge perfectionism
     B. Take risks and act
     C. Act "as if" and let go
     D. Cultivate a growth mindset
     E. Use the power of intention

Take Action: Experiment and consider these questions

Courageous leadership is risky and requires confidence. It is critical to be clear about what's important to you, and to be willing to live with the consequences of the risks you take. Part of my role in coaching and consulting is to be a "thought partner" to others, asking hard questions that require reasoning as well as listening to your heart. Here are some questions for you to think about and consider:

1. Does perfectionism play a big role in my life? How might I let go of being overly focused on making things perfect?
2. What are the risks involved in taking a stance I'd like to advance in my life or work? Do the benefits outweigh the possible downside?
3. What could acting "as if" look like if I felt even more confident in a certain situation?
4. How can I bolster my confidence so that I can act on what I know is right?
5. What are my intentions for myself? others? How are they playing out in my life?

If you are able to gain some insight and define a next step for yourself that requires courage, take heart. You identified your direction. Acting courageously doesn't always feel good. In fact, it's often frightening, or at least uncomfortable. But you can do it.

It's time to jump into the deep water and trust that you can swim.

There is no greater gift you can give
or receive than to honor your calling.
It's why you were born.

Oprah Winfrey

Chapter 2:

Right Focus — Your Personal and Professional Compass

When I first met Holly, she didn't yet realize just how badly she needed a career change. Holly held a senior director's position with a large, publicly traded company. Her work focused on marketing strategy and sales in the technology space. She was good at it, but she wasn't fulfilled. Holly felt worn down by the marketing analysis work she did; the unreasonable deadlines and the culture of bureaucracy that complicated her effectiveness. It wasn't until Holly's participation in the Key Women's Leadership Forum that she began to ask herself questions like "Why am I so unhappy in my position?" and "What do I really want—what am I passionate about?"

Holly felt trapped in her job. She is a single parent and the main source of support for her teenage daughter. She and her daughter were beginning to look at colleges. The thought of leaving her well-paid position with health benefits to do something else was overwhelming.

In our forum, the women devote time to getting in touch with what enlivens them. As part of that exploration, Holly brought the issue of feeling stuck and not being fulfilled in her work to the women. During the questioning phase, one woman asked Holly if she ever considered becoming an entrepreneur. Holly once thought about starting her own business many years ago while in college. A long time elapsed since pondering it last, but that question triggered Holly's memory. She remembered how much she loved baking cookies and arranging them in creative ways. She saw in her mind's eye cookies in colorful letters, word puzzles, and even company logos.

Holly's great grandmother, Bess, was a baker. With the untimely death of her husband, Bess needed to work to support her young daughter. She, her brother and her sister opened their first bakery in 1916. The family-owned bakery developed a reputation for excellence and eventually grew to 13 locations throughout the Pittsburgh area.

Holly inherited the baking gene from her great-grandmother. She loved to make cookies, especially around the holidays. Her family and friends raved about her delicious, attractively decorated cookies.

Holly also studied communications and marketing and earned her MBA before starting her first corporate job at a Fortune 500 company. It was during the early years of that first job that she had an idea for a cookie business. She had even started to formulate plans for what products she would offer and how she would market herself. Being a young professional quickly moving up the ranks, she nonetheless tucked the idea away and focused on her career. Life moved on. She married, had a child, and continued working. Holly and her husband divorced when her daughter was three. Afterwards, Holly shouldered most of the responsibility for parenting while juggling the demands of a career that appeared successful.

Now, those ideas for a business all came back to her.

"What if I left my demanding job and started my own cookie-baking company?" she asked herself. Then reality set in and she stopped day-dreaming. She dutifully returned to her corporate job. Holly continued in her day-to-day routine, feeling torn between her passion and her responsibilities.

 # What we know

Many women are busy trying to meet others' needs or expectations at work and at home. They often don't invest the time they need in themselves to discover who they are, what brings them joy, and how to create success for themselves in the world. Take Eleanor, for example. She works at an accounting firm where she is often asked to work late due to client workload. She has two young children as well as a sick grandmother for whom she provides care. Her husband helps with chores, but she is the one who oversees the management of the household, primarily because she's better at it. Between competing demands from her boss and family, the idea of taking time to reflect on what's truly purposeful for her seems foreign, even selfish.

Most of us want to derive satisfaction and meaning from our work. Making money alone isn't the goal. In Gallup's surveys, as well as others, the highest-rated motivators across industries involve finding challenging or meaningful work (Pendell). Work becomes engaging when it sparks our passion, plays to our strengths, and fits our values.

One of the ways to discover meaning and build lasting confidence is to go inside and get clarity on what is purposeful for you. Whether you are in a position to act immediately on your direction, or if you need a longer-range plan and the time to get there, the first step is identifying your personal purpose. As Bill George stated in his book *True North*, it's important to find your direction and align with it. Your "true north" is the point that orients you—it gives you stability in a complex world. It is your internal compass and represents you at the deepest level.

In the book *The Power of Purpose*, Richard Leider discusses the importance of learning to live from the inside out. The life we live isn't fulfilling until we discover our passion as well as our gifts and how to apply them. By aligning your personal passion with your talent, you enhance the quality of your life, and ultimately that of others' lives. In Kevin McCarthy's *The On-Purpose Person*, a character describes life with purpose as "a sense of sheer joy and divine pleasure, regardless of the difficulty or ease of what I was doing. Energy and life flowed because I was in a zone of alignment—like I was a conduit for something greater than I was." (12) McCarthy outlines a process of setting priorities to support your purpose by recommending that you compare them with each other and select those that are most important to work on, and that ultimately advance your living a purposeful life. Below, I offer my own process for finding purpose, one that uses effective strategic planning principles that have enlivened the lives of many we've coached, particularly women.

 # We could use new framing

In this chapter, I outline a process I developed in my coaching practice called Right Focus that helps you get clarity on what's purposeful and the best direction for you.

Through the strategic planning work done with executive teams and organizations over the years, I've witnessed the power of answering some simple yet powerful questions about your team or organization:

- Who are we? Why do we exist?
- What do we stand for?
- Where do we see ourselves going?
- How will we get there?

Right Focus culminates with an agreed-upon mission, values, vision, and plan. Discovering answers to these questions gets everyone rowing in the same direction, and excited about anticipated results.

In coaching others one-on-one, I've prompted my clients to ask themselves the same questions. People got excited about what they discovered about themselves and especially about the clarity they received in their lives.

Right Focus transforms the ordinary into the extraordinary. It allows you to create the space within your life to be part of something bigger. Right Focus consists of:

- Defining your mission (why are you here)
- Clarifying your values (what you stand for)
- Establishing your vision (where you see yourself going)
- Identifying your strengths and core focus (what you can be best at)

Taking the time to craft an inspirational and accurate mission, values, vision, and core focus is your chance to create powerful significance for yourself. When your personal mission, values, vision, and core focus are accurate and aligned with your work, you are centered, energized, and productive. Understanding yourself at the core makes you a better leader, partner, and parent; it also increases your chances to live a fulfilling life. Let's take a look at each part of Right Focus.

Mission

Your mission is your higher calling. It is the motivating force that underlies everything you do—your reason for being. A mission is a brief statement of your personal purpose. It is a description of what inspires you and motivates you at the deepest levels. Your mission statement answers questions like: "What am I here to do with my life?", "What is it that makes me feel alive?", and "What is the essence of my passion and motivation?"

An ideal mission statement offers a sense of meaningful direction. Having a clearly stated mission acts as a compass to help you focus your energy into staying on a path that leads you to success and ultimately, happiness.

A strong mission statement has the following characteristics:

- Clear enough to be easily understood and communicated.
- Brief enough to be easily remembered.
- Inspiring enough to encourage others to want to support you. This means it must contain an element of being of service to others in some way.
- Broad enough to encompass your innate talents and abilities.
- Authentic enough that anyone who knows you well would agree.
- Timeless enough to be accurate throughout your life—there is no deadline on it.

Values

Values are your core set of guiding principles, the things that are so important to you that they cannot be compromised for profit or financial gain—no matter what. "What do I stand for?", "What is most important to me?", and "What is my code of ethics?" are key values questions. Knowing your values helps you make better decisions.

Getting clarity on your own values is a critical step in becoming an effective leader. The best and most inspiring leaders have a consistent set of values that they display every day. In other words, leaders do what they say is important—they model what they stand for (Bennis).

While working on our book *CEO Road Rules: Right Focus, Right People, Right Execution*, my co-author Dennis Stearns and I interviewed business leaders who succeeded in doing just that. One of the people we spoke to was Michael Dougherty, the former CEO of Kindermusik, a music and movement program serving children and families around the globe. Dougherty shared that he has three core values that he emphasizes in his business, with his family, and in working on community projects: Be Open, Honest, and Direct—OHD for short. His board, executives, co-workers, and family hear one or all three mentioned just about every week.

Dougherty speaks of these values frequently and gives examples of putting them into practice or failing to do so. As a result, those around him on a daily basis as well as the thousands of teachers worldwide who met with him or talked to him on the phone know his values. They often respond by being more open, honest, and direct in their own dealings with him and his company than they might otherwise have been. Clarity about your values helps you and those around you to be more transparent in your communication.

Vision

Vision is a critical part of Right Focus because it describes your preferred future and becomes your overriding long-term goal. Vision answers questions like: "Where do I see myself going?" and "Where do I want to be in the next five to ten years?"

A vision differs from a mission. A mission statement describes the purpose of the person, team, or organization and is not an overriding goal that, once achieved, changes. Mission statements usually last for a lifetime. The vision sets a direction you can track and measure. Once you realize your vision, it's time to create a new one in order to keep growing.

A good example of the distinction between a personal mission and a vision is in the 1985 movie *Back to the Future*. When the movie opens and Marty McFly (Michael J. Fox) enters Professor Emmett Brown's home, we see that the professor has clocks and gadgets hooked up to move together precisely at the top of the hour and open a dog food can to feed Einstein, the professor's dog. We know before ever meeting the professor that he loves to invent things. It becomes very clear over the course of the movie that the professor's mission or purpose in life is to invent.

As the plot expands, we learn that Professor Brown has a clear vision for his next invention: to be the first person to explore the past and future and be able to return to the present—time travel. He accomplishes this vision and he and McFly share some fun and dangerous adventures traveling through time. The professor used his passion for inventing to fuel his vision of traveling across time. Once he achieved his vision of time travel, he goes on to invent other things in the future.

The movie example is a contrived plot. When the women in our Key Women's Leadership Forum identify their missions and visions, it's a powerful process that serves as a guidepost going forward in their lives. One of our participants, a chief medical officer, defined her mission as "building teams that do incredible things." Her vision is to "create a high-performance team that takes cancer research to the next level."

Core Focus

Core focus is about knowing what key talents, strengths, or competencies you bring to the table that enable you to excel in the world. Without a core focus, it's easy to get excited about new possibilities and become sidetracked instead of developing what you can be best at in your world. Once you are clear about your core strengths, it's equally important that you build on them and develop them to their fullest potential.

In our efforts to learn and develop ourselves, we face the temptation to veer into realms that are not our core strengths. Spending too much time and effort in a non-core area interferes with your ability to build your core focus. Oftentimes, people elect to spend more time on trying to improve a weakness instead of developing core strength.

On a personal level, suppose your core focus or strength is helping people manage their finances via better budgeting and investing. Along the way you learn some spreadsheet software skills. Should you veer from your path to develop custom budgeting software yourself? Or would it be better to partner with someone who has that core competency and let them do it?

There are cases where you might find a previously undiscovered passion that warrants pursuing and may lead to a new focus. However, if you already determined a core focus at which you excel and are passionate about, the process of seeking new ones may result in diluting yourself. Chances are you will not create the best budgeting software out there. By trying, you may undermine your ability to be the best advisor and financial management consultant. Your time may be better spent figuring out how you can develop your core strength—build on it, bring it to new audiences, and parlay past successes into future wins.

4 Strategies to Seize Success and Develop Right Focus

Below is a set of strategies to develop your personal mission, values, vision, and core focus. Select which ones to work on or develop all four. As you read, see which actions appeal to you as an approach you can experiment with to gain clarity on your internal compass.

Action A: Develop your personal mission

The best and most inspiring mission statements are broad and authentic; they capture the essence of what drives you to contribute to the world. Your mission statement should include a strong action verb, such as "build" versus "try to develop"; the verb serves as a container of sorts for what sparks your passion in life.

Some examples of effective personal mission statements include:

- To create beautiful environments for myself and others in which to blossom.
- To make people laugh and have fun so they can reduce stress.
- To serve others and live my spiritual beliefs every day.

One way to dig deeper and get to the true essence of your personal mission is to ask yourself "What" questions that help you get to the core of your mission. For example, you could ask yourself:

- "What is motivating me when I do…?"
- "What is important about that?"
- "What is appealing about…?"

Ask yourself at least three "what" questions after you come up with the first draft of your mission statement. As an example, let's consider a woman I coached named Susan, and the process we used to identify her personal mission statement.

Referred to me a few years ago, Susan sought support because her career lacked direction. During the Mission exercise, Susan noticed that she felt most energized and passionate whenever she decorated spaces. At school, at work, at home, and even at friends' homes, she often decorated and rearranged spaces. This pattern started in grade school and never stopped! She particularly loved decorating homes. She logically concluded that her passion and mission were to decorate homes for people. But was that her real deep mission? Is there a greater purpose we can uncover?

Susan delved into "The Three Whats" to get to that deeper, more purposeful mission statement. Here's how it went.

Susan	Coach
My mission is to decorate homes for people.	What is motivating you when you decorate homes?
I love the process of creating beauty and harmony out of dull, lifeless spaces.	What is important about creating beauty and harmony?
When spaces are beautiful and harmonious people feel happier and more relaxed and hopefully it helps to make their families happier, too.	What is appealing about helping people feel happier?
I feel like I'm making a difference in peoples' lives and helping to create positive energy in the world.	So, what is your deeper purpose and mission in life?
My mission is to create beauty, harmony, and positive energy that make a difference in peoples' lives.	Excellent!

By digging deeper, you reveal a personal mission broad enough and flexible enough to give you room to expand and grow in the ways that fulfill your mission. Your mission is purposeful enough and big enough to inspire you and the people around you, even when the going gets tough.

In Susan's case, her mission became much larger than helping people with decorating their homes. She started there, and later expanded her work to include office spaces, schools, community centers, and any activities that create beauty for Susan and the people she helps. Her broader mission statement allows for bigger and more varied things to happen in Susan's life because creating beauty and positive energy doesn't always take the form of interior decorating. It could include landscaping, fashion, Feng shui, or myriad other activities Susan finds fulfilling.

The end result of this exercise is a more compelling and accurate personal mission—one that can stand the test of time and be consistent throughout your life.

It's important to get your mission statement defined because it also serves as a reference point to make sure you are on track and focusing on what's really important in life. If you start to feel out of balance, stop and ask yourself, "Is what I'm doing purposeful for me? Does this really fit my mission?" If you answered "no" to any of these, keep returning to the previous steps until they all apply.

 ## Action B: Develop personal values

Values are your core set of guiding principles, a statement of what is so important to you that it cannot be compromised for material gain. The key questions that guide you to your values are: "What do I stand for?" and "What is most important to me?"

Knowing your values helps you make better decisions. Knowing what's really important assists you in assessing alternatives and choosing the one that's the best fit for you. Your confidence in making decisions grows when you are aware of your core values.

Getting clarity on your own values is a critical step in becoming an effective leader. Your personal values should align with those of your team and your organization for you to feel like you belong there. For example, one of our forum participants has as one of her personal values, "Quality and achieving a high standard of excellence in all I do." When she took a position with a company that valued speed and doing the bare minimum to get the product out the door fast (they called this "efficiency"), she became frustrated. Her personal values were not aligned with the company—they were in conflict.

Identifying your personal values involves examining the relative importance of the things you hold dear. Consider the list of values below. Review the list; add any values that you don't see listed that you consider important. Identify your top 10 values:

- ☐ ACHIEVEMENT (sense of accomplishment; setting goals and reaching them)
- ☐ ADVANCEMENT (moving forward in my career through promotions)
- ☐ ADVENTURE (work which frequently involves risk taking or travel)
- ☐ AESTHETICS (involved in studying or appreciating the beauty of ideas, things, etc.)
- ☐ AUTONOMY (work independently, determine my work without a lot of direction from others)
- ☐ CARING (love, affection)
- ☐ CHALLENGE (stimulates full use of your potential)
- ☐ CHANGE & VARIETY (varied, frequently changing work responsibilities and/or work settings)
- ☐ COMPETITION (my abilities against those of others where there is a clear win/lose outcome)
- ☐ COOPERATION (opportunity to work as a team toward common goals)
- ☐ CREATIVITY (being imaginative, innovative, coming up with ideas)
- ☐ ECONOMIC SECURITY (having enough money)

- ☐ EXCITEMENT (experience a high degree of, or frequent excitement in your work)
- ☐ FAMILY HAPPINESS (being able to spend quality time and develop relationships with family)
- ☐ FRIENDSHIP (develop close personal relationships)
- ☐ HEALTH (physical and psychological well-being)
- ☐ HELP OTHERS (be involved in helping people in a direct way, individually or in a group)
- ☐ HELP SOCIETY (do something to contribute to improve the world)
- ☐ INNER HARMONY (being at peace with oneself)
- ☐ INTEGRITY (sincerity and honesty)
- ☐ INTELLECTUAL STATUS (be regarded as an expert in my field, seen as smart)
- ☐ KNOWLEDGE (understanding gained through study and experience)
- ☐ LEADERSHIP (influence over others, rather lead than follow)
- ☐ LEISURE (have time for hobbies, sports, activities, and interests)
- ☐ LOCATION (live somewhere that will fit my lifestyle/allows me to do the things I enjoy most)
- ☐ LOYALTY (steadfastness and allegiance)
- ☐ PLEASURE (enjoyment)
- ☐ POWER (authority, control)
- ☐ PRECISION (work in situations where there is little tolerance for error)
- ☐ RESPONSIBILITY (being accountable for results)
- ☐ RECOGNITION (getting acknowledged for your contribution)
- ☐ STABILITY (steady work routine and predictable duties, not likely to change)
- ☐ SPIRITUALITY (feel connected to a presence larger than myself and to a oneness with others)
- ☐ TIME FREEDOM (flexible work schedule, no specific work hours required)
- ☐ WEALTH (profit, gain, make a lot of money)
- ☐ WISDOM (accumulation of knowledge)

*Modified from an exercise provided by and with the permission of The Institute for Professional Excellence in Coaching (iPEC)

Next, prioritize the values that you selected, with 1 being most important and 10 being the least among your top 10. As you do so, review your list again and ask yourself:

- Which of these values are essential to me and guide all my decisions and behaviors?
- Which are important, but don't have as much weight in my life?
- Are there any that I should drop because they don't reflect what I hold dear through my behaviors and actions?

Action C: Develop your personal vision

Vision is your picture of a preferred reality, your highest and best dreams for yourself. It answers the question: "If my highest wishes for myself were realized in the next five… ten… twenty years, what would I see?"

To determine your *personal* vision, consider the following additional questions:

1. Describe your personal and work life now (situation at work, home, how you spend your time, current goals, etc.).
2. Ask yourself what your life would be like in five to ten or twenty years if future events in your professional and personal life were successful and fulfilling?
3. If success were assured, what would you want to accomplish in your life? What would you be or do?

Take time to write a narrative of your picture of success. What are the common themes you see as you answer the above questions? These themes are fuel for developing your long -range goals. Here are some examples:

- To get my novels published and have one become a bestseller.
- To become president of our company in 7 years.

- To build community through the development of a joint vision and execution of a plan that takes us to a new level of growth at the end of the decade.

There's a tool we use in the Key Women's Leadership Forum to increase the chances of a participant's dreams becoming reality. It's called the Performance Letter. If you were guaranteed that two-thirds of what you put into a letter addressed to yourself would become reality, would you try it? That's the concept behind writing a Performance Letter. I polled CEO and Key Leader groups I worked with over the past twenty years informally. The general consensus across over 100 people is that about 66% of what they projected for their future year when put in the Performance Letter format came into being. So how does this work?

Most people in leadership roles work off a business and sometimes a personal development plan of some sort. Plans are linear and "left brain" in their function. Left-brain thinking is analytical and verbal. By adding a vivid description of how your year has gone as if it has already happened, you access the right brain. Right-brain thinking is intuitive and visual. The power of this approach comes from using both approaches in planning your year and your longer-term vision. When you use multiple capacities of the brain, you enhance the chances that your preferred future will become reality.

Here are the basic steps to write your Performance Letter:

1. Date the letter one year in advance: December 31, 20__. Create a vivid description of your career and life at that point in time: where you are, how you arrived there, and why you chose your particular path. Include as much detail as possible—more details mean a greater likelihood of success. In other words, write a letter to your current self from your future self, as if one year's worth of future events had already happened.
2. Describe your long-term vision and how your one-year letter advances it.
3. Talk about how you grew as a leader. Include a section on your personal growth and development and your plan to achieve those

goals. What are some of the activities in which you engaged? Who assisted you?

4. Include how you feel physically, emotionally, mentally, and spiritually. It's also helpful to write a personal section on the relationships that are important to you.

5. Read your letter often (monthly) and picture it unfolding in your mind's eye. Make adjustments to the letter as needed so that it still rings true when you review it.

The goal of writing a Performance Letter is to visualize yourself achieving your highest and best for yourself and others. The average letter is from two to three pages. Once finished, you'll have a perfect personal development plan template. I usually start mine with the phrase: "It's been a wonderful year of work success, strong relationships, and fun."

Here's an excerpt from one of our member's letter to give you a sense of what a Performance Letter is like:

"You're thriving. You connect with your sense of purpose daily. That purpose is to nurture yourself to be your highest self, and to nurture others towards the same. Your highest self leads with compassion and openness to possibility without feeling a need to control outcomes. You walk in the direction of your dreams, focusing on the journey more than the destination.

Your direction will lead you to a time where you are able to work from anywhere—meaningfully contributing to a variety of projects and people, while maintaining a healthy, active lifestyle and financial strength for the necessities plus new experiences, like travel. In your ideal place, you're able to hike more, focus more, and create more.

Your company is growing again. Your new approach of tightly integrating marketing with sales enablement is in place and the reorganization of the team is complete. The new private equity owners have tapped the marketing team as the new gold standard for marketing planning and reporting and would like us to share our best practices with the other companies in their portfolio. The team feels happy, optimistic, accomplished and proud—they have a sense of meaning. More than this professional accomplishment, you're happy to see the sense of achievement and satisfaction in your team members and with the interns you mentor.

You also got back into the classroom again as a guest lecturer. This is where your passion for marketing comes through and the energy multiplies with students who share it. This is laying the foundation for going back to teaching full-time in five years."

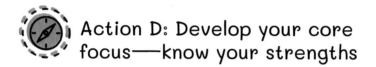

Action D: Develop your core focus—know your strengths

Core focus is about knowing what your key talents and strengths are.

To determine your personal core focus, consider asking yourself (and others): "What am I or can I be best at in my world?" The answer to this question positions you to excel in a key area that plays to your strengths. Having a clear core focus gives you a competitive advantage. It allows you to concentrate your time and energy on where your talents are and helps you differentiate yourself. Core focus helps you to build your personal brand — what you are known for providing. Since building a core focus involves setting priorities, you can improve life balance for yourself and those you care about.

Your core focus statement is a brief statement of your personal strengths, talents, and what you are best at doing. The following questions can assist you in gaining clarity about your core focus. Don't try to be perfect, simply write what comes to mind! You may also want to interview people you live and work with and see how they perceive what you are best at in your world. List everything you can think of.

Here are some areas to cover:

My greatest talents are:
My personal strengths include:
People often compliment me on:

Now go back and review your answers to the above questions. Share them with a couple of trusted friends, family members, and people you admire to see if they have anything to add.

As you review the answers, think about which of them you not only are good at, but also really love. Which are you passionate about? Which of these strengths make you feel alive and engaged when using them?

The Gallup organization has extensive research on identifying your unique strengths (gallupstrengthscenter.com). I recommend that you take their assessment to help you further identify your core focus.

 ## Seizing Success: Holly's Story

After the conversation Holly had with the forum members about starting a business, she initially rejected the idea and decided to continue making the best of her marketing job. She continued to think about her personal passion, communicating caring through baking.

Fear gripped her. Holly stayed in limbo for the next year and continued to explore her idea and the anxiety she felt in our forum. "Why would I, a single parent, want to leave a high-paying job with benefits to try to be the next Mrs. Fields?" she asked the women rhetorically.

Gradually, an answer emerged: The business idea was worth trying because it aligned with her mission and core values in a way her current job would never match. With the group's support, Holly dipped her toe in the water and started baking on the side. She brought in wonderful cookies for all of us to enjoy, and even made gluten-free ones for those of us who are gluten-intolerant. Some of the women in the forum hired her to make cookies for corporate events. Holly got serious about resurrecting her business plan from long ago. She put her marketing skills to use and began bringing in bigger and bigger orders. Now her business focuses on word messages of all kinds, from "Happy Sweet 16" to "Congratulations on your retirement." She also transforms her cookies into corporate logos for high-profile business events.

The confluence of the encouragement from the group, her passion for baking, and the example of other female entrepreneurs with families in the forum helped Holly to make the leap. In 2016, she started her own "confectionary communications company," Eatyourwordscookies.com, a century after her great-grandmother Bess started hers.

You don't have to leave what you are currently doing or venture out as an entrepreneur to have Right Focus. Many women who don't want to make a dramatic change still benefit from learning what best fits them and adjusting their work and life to be more reflective of their mission, values, vision, and core focus.

 ## Review the four growth strategies in this chapter

Using the growth strategies will assist you in defining what you are passionate about and your guiding principles as well as clarifying where you see yourself going, and what your strengths are.

    A. Developing your personal mission.
    B. Developing your personal values.
    C. Developing your personal vision.
    D. Developing your core focus.

Take Action: Experiment and consider these questions

Right Focus is the compass that helps you understand yourself at a deeper level and clarifies the best direction for you. It will guide you in times of uncertainty and help you make the best decisions for you. Here are the main questions:

1. Who am I? What is my purpose?
2. What do I value? What are the guiding principles that I won't compromise?
3. Where do I see myself going? What's the highest and best I see for myself in the future?
4. What are the strengths and talents I bring to my work? How can I build on them?
5. What is the plan I picture to guide me over the next year and beyond?

It's not what other people believe you can do —
it's what you believe you can do.

Gail Devers

Chapter 3:

Pressure to Perform — Building Resilience

A s a computer engineer, Morgan had a strong track record of successfully leading complex projects. In one assignment, to assess the company's cybersecurity vulnerability, she led a team of 24 people across the US to document the current state of the system and make recommendations for addressing possible security breaches. Company leaders noticed how well the project went and offered her a new role as senior project manager for a multi-million-dollar initiative on the use of Bitcoin in her company. Her new team included 56 people around the globe, including a former colleague who also wanted the position. After the initial glow of accomplishment, Morgan started to feel tremendous pressure to be successful in leading the team, as well as in meeting the agreed-upon goals of the project.

Although her former peer, Collin, didn't initially seem resistant, she started to observe a lot of push-back from him. Morgan invited Collin to have coffee and discuss the scope of the work and his responsibilities.

She asked for his help and was taken by surprise at how Collin viewed her promotion: "You didn't deserve it. I have far more experience in this area than you and they gave it to you because our company wants more women in technology-driven projects. Now you're coming to me!" Morgan politely listened to Collin and reiterated her request for his support. Collin looked at her without expression.

Morgan didn't know how to handle Collin's reaction, or how to eventually engage him. She hesitated in dealing with Collin and found herself second-guessing her approach with the rest of the team. Morgan succeeded on her last project because she was willing to try new things. Now she found herself stuck. The pressure to perform paralyzed her at times.

Morgan didn't feel she could go to her superiors for advice about how to handle Collin for fear of looking weak. The company culture was all about getting things done. Morgan's boss liked to say "learn by fire." Morgan didn't have much practice in exerting her authority over team members who didn't trust her. For women like Morgan, the need for better collaboration and support can divert their focus from taking needed action.

 ## What we know

In the business world, pressure, stakes, and high standards are supposed to drive excellent performance. With what I've seen working with executive women, however, the opposite is often true for them. They may experience the pressure their peers and superiors place on them as a heavy burden or an expectation of perfection they can't possibly meet. It doesn't help that some male executives, like Collin, are hyper-critical of, and even hostile to, female leaders. The reality is even more complex than that.

Studies of differences in how the sexes respond to performance challenges show that males are encouraged to "get back in the game" more often than are females. There are also gender differences in risk-taking—men under stress are more likely to take risks than they would be otherwise, while women under stress become more reluctant to do so (Mather and Lighthall).

In a recent series of experiments, sociologists Sheryl Ball, Catherine Eckel, and Maria Heracleous asked individuals to make risky decisions for themselves and to predict the risky decisions of others. The women in the experiment were more averse to taking risks and less likely to believe that others would make risky decisions. The researchers further investigated whether physical differences such as strength, height, and attractiveness make a difference in perception. Overall, they found that physically stronger and taller people and those perceived as attractive are more risk-tolerant. Since women tend to be smaller and weaker than men, this can also be a factor in making women fear risk.

The reason that many women tend to stay in the safe zone isn't provided by research, but it's easy to guess. Males receive the message that mistakes are inevitable and resiliency is to be prized. Females report getting the message that they need to do it right and make everything okay for others. This message starts early and is persistent. One member of our Key Women's Leadership Forum summed it up well when she recalled that her mom reprimanded her when her homework was less than perfect while her brother seemed exempt just as long as he "tried." As Kay and Shipman write in *The Confidence Code*, it's in elementary school that "you'll find the insidious seeds of society's gender imbalance; because it's there that we were first rewarded for being good, instead of energetic, rambunctious, or even pushy" (87). Women in challenging situations fear making a mistake, and this impacts performance.

 # We could use new framing

The typical ways high-achieving women relate to performance pressure and striving for success include working themselves to exhaustion, demanding perfection of themselves, and trying to please everyone – a tough, if not impossible feat. Compound all of this with shouldering family obligations, feeling guilty that they can't be present for loved ones as much as they want, and having a fear of failure and it's no wonder many women are risk averse and prone to burnout.

Pressure to perform takes many forms. The feeling that there "aren't enough hours in the day" can create stress leading to deteriorating performance and personal repercussions. At one of our Key Women's Leadership Forums, one participant, "Stacey," reflected on how she worked over the Thanksgiving holiday to get a high-stakes project done. Not only did she feel the stress of the deadline, but she keenly felt the disappointment of her family. Emotions stoked the pressure of the task and made it even harder to handle.

When others around them experience negative emotions, women often feel the need to manage those feelings, act as a sounding board, or provide some solution to help the other party feel better. Those others include disgruntled colleagues like Collin, whom Morgan felt pressured to win over. They can also include family members, bosses, clients, and just about anyone else with whom we come into contact.

My colleague, Dr. Hank Weisinger, and his co-author, JP Pawliw-Fry, conducted research on over six thousand women and shared their findings in their bestselling book *Performing Under Pressure*. They report that women face a significant "second layer of pressure" in the workplace. The second layer consists of:

- Having too much to do with not enough time
- Managing change
- Balancing work-life priorities

Women still assume the responsibilities of managing the household far more than men. They usually take the lead on caring for the children, and if they are a single mom, they must manage all of the responsibilities. A past Forbes poll revealed that 63% of working mothers agree with the statement: "Sometimes I feel like a married single mom" (Herrick). The lack of awareness and skills to handle this added pressure impedes a woman's ability to perform in an organization. Falling off the career track is often the result.

Every employee wants to do well, but women face a variety of added pressures that aren't there for men. Morgan put pressure on herself to be liked by every team member and to handle her clash with Collin without going to anyone else for help. Stacey felt pressure to prove her dedication by working over a holiday but also felt guilt from her family when she did so. Have you experienced similar pressures?

A survey we completed in 2016 in Tampa Bay underscores how pervasive the pressure to perform is among women. In our survey, about 50% of our 105 female executive respondents reported that pressure to perform is the foremost or second most important challenge in their careers. Comments in the survey often reflected that women feel a greater need to prove themselves at work.

How do women cope with this pressure? Too often, by giving in—accepting the idea that they're responsible for every outcome, and must work harder to please everyone and create perfect outcomes. After Collin questioned Morgan's skill, she started second-guessing key decisions she made, worrying that any misstep would prove his criticisms were true.

☆ 5 Strategies to Seize Success While Handling Pressure To Perform

Here are five effective approaches to managing pressure to perform. These techniques turn down the dial on your fear, help you accept the reality of imperfection, and connect you with the skills and abilities you already have. As you read, see which appeal to you as an approach with which you can experiment.

Action A: Embrace what you fear and make it a game

Pressure to perform entwines deeply with fear. When you feel pressured, you feel scared of the repercussions of not living up to expectations. Fearful thinking undermines your self-confidence, diminishes your energy, and negatively affects your health.

Approaching a situation as a mental game can take the fear out of the equation. When you start to experience fear in a situation, notice how it makes you feel and ask yourself why. Don't judge yourself—just answer the internal question. Then picture yourself helicoptering over the situation and watching it as if you were an impartial observer. Some call this third-person observer your "witness self." In this mode you see the situation objectively. You envision all the possible ways you could react and make a guess about the likely results of each. For instance, what if Morgan laughed off Collin's complaints? Lectured him to show more respect? Asked to have him removed from the team? Some of these might be the wrong choice, but considering the options dispassionately helps you see possibilities that might otherwise intimidate you.

Reframe your thinking and see the situation at a distance. Once detached, make it a challenge, even a game. Let me tell you more about what this could look like.

Case Study: Jason

I studied "exposure therapy" during my psychology training. This is a technique that helps people who avoid objects, activities, or situations they're uncomfortable with by systematically exposing them to what they fear in a safe environment. Reading about Jason Comely, an IT professional from Ontario who feared rejection, reminded me about the importance of facing, even embracing, what we fear most. Jason didn't realize that he used this technique on himself—but the real surprise was it worked.

Jason decided to force himself to do the thing he feared most, be rejected by others on a daily basis. Whether it involved asking for a date or asking to borrow money, he made rejection into a game. He did so by making himself approach others and make absurd or unlikely requests like "Can I help you clean your house?" Jason expected to get rejected, so he knew that it wouldn't crush him. By making daily low-stakes requests, he learned to approach people and became more approachable in turn. Sometimes people granted his requests, other times not. Eventually, he wrote down his rejection attempts and made them into a deck of cards he sells online, the Rejection Therapy game. People all around the world have joined in on the rejection game.

What do you avoid because in the short term it's more comfortable not to do it? We all have something, whether it's speaking to a large audience or presenting ideas to authority figures. The problem is that avoidance in the short term negatively impacts your long-term goals, such as being an effective and inspiring CEO or senior-level executive. For Morgan, confronting her team member Collin, who challenged her authority, was her fear. By avoiding him, she impeded her long-term goal of proving her managerial and leadership skills over a large team. What if instead she challenged herself to start two conversations with him each day, using a friendly, upbeat, and assertive tone? He might have seen she wasn't intimidated by him and backed down.

Action B: Recall a past success

Let's return to Morgan and her fear that she won't be effective leading her team. One strategy to handle the pressure is to recall herself at her best. She might ask herself: "When did I lead a successful project in the past, and how did that feel?"

The strategy is to think back to a specific time when you were successful. By continuing to remind yourself that you have been successful leading projects, speaking in public, or developing ideas, you build your confidence, even under challenging circumstances. For Morgan, it was her success leading the cybersecurity project. She remembered all the smart decisions she made with input from her team and how good it felt to use her creativity to solve problems.

While we're in the midst of a challenge, it feels like a unique hurdle. Instead of labeling the moment as "do or die," see it as something you've done in a similar situation in the past and can do again. Research suggests that thoughts and feelings associated with past experiences stay with you, whether they are positive or negative. Research by neuropsychologists Katherine Duncan and Daphna Shohamy examined the power of this process. The team had students play a game in which they were shown pairs of cards and rewarded with cash for choosing the correct one. Later, they received a different task in which they chose between pairs of images but received no reward. The students tended to pick the "correct" images from the earlier game. The positive associations with those images lingered—even when the subjects had no detailed recollection of the earlier task (Duncan and Shohamy).

Duncan and Shohamy point out that we're often guided in our decisions by this type of "episodic memory," as opposed to just by our abstract values. That might sound less than ideal—we'd all like to think our choices are rational. You can use this dynamic to your advantage by purposely calling up a positive memory relevant to a given task. Accessing positive feelings about things you accomplished in the past actually changes the chemistry of your brain. Your confidence improves and you become more productive.

Of course, some challenges really are unique and hard to respond to perfectly. I'm not advocating that you make unreasonable demands of yourself. I'm recommending that when you have an unavoidable challenge and feel negative pressure or resentment building, you change the way you think and feel about it. It's very likely that the situation will improve. The women in our forums report great results using this strategy ranging from making high stakes presentations to predicting trends confidently in strategic planning sessions.

Action C: Breathe and find the right word

My colleague Dr. Taryn Morgan is the assistant director of Athletic and Personal Development at IMG Academy in Bradenton, Florida and is a brilliant coach. She has a doctorate in Sports Psychology and helps to oversee 50 staff members who train athletes in physical conditioning, mental conditioning, leadership, athletic training, vision training, and nutrition. As a coach, she teaches athletes to "make friends with the moment" and see each roadblock as a challenge. When I asked her guidance, she shared some tips that can help you to thrive under pressure.

1. Simply take a deep breath. In the nose for at least 4 seconds, pause, out the mouth for at least 4 seconds. And not the one where your shoulders and chest rise (that's a shallow breath), but the deep kind. If you put your hands on your belly button, you should feel your belly expand when you breathe in and then fall back when you breathe out. Breathing is the best way to promote relaxation and calm. Take a few deep breaths as a reset when you feel pressure.

2. Look at the situation objectively and find your focus word. What can you do to be successful in the situation? Think of the simplest thing that answers the question, "HOW do I perform well?" This helps bring laser focus to the situation and makes it seem much more manageable. For example, if you need to execute a second

serve in tennis, you may remind yourself "SPIN" so that you get enough spin on the serve. Don't say, "don't double fault" or "don't miss" or "I have to make this" or "this serve has so much pressure," because those would all cause you to get tense.

3. Remember your training and tell yourself, "Pressure is only there if I put it there" or "I love pressure" or even "This is fun." Any of these reminders help you keep the situation and the pressure (which is actually just put there by your thoughts) in perspective. You can also use positive self-talk to remind yourself that "I can do this" or "I'm prepared for this."

Taryn shared a success story with me about a figure skater she coached. I'll call her Gwen. In their first meeting, Gwen was very nervous, and the thought of competing at the highest levels made her sick. "I have a hard time seeing myself as an Olympian," she admitted. It was obvious to Taryn that despite Gwen's significant talent, she needed to bolster her confidence and find a system to minimize her stress. The pair worked together to identify ways Gwen could stay calmer and more poised under pressure. Gwen used the breathing, focus words, and power statements I have just described.

Previously, while Gwen executed her axel jumps in training perfectly, she tended to falter when she attempted the challenging jumps in competition. She lost points for awkward landings and even fell a few times. As she began to train her brain to keep a balanced perspective, Gwen developed a new mindset. She had bouts with self-doubt along the way but continued to remind herself, "I can do this." She became more and more able to land the jumps in competition, and instead of making costly mistakes, she began executing her routine flawlessly. She wound up qualifying for the Olympics by .02 of a point and placed in the top 10 of her event.

Gwen's dream became reality when she adopted a new way of managing internal pressure. She now coaches other figure skaters and partners with Taryn to help them to build that same type of resilience.

Case Study: Brenda

One of the women in our Key Women's Leadership Forum adopted a similar approach to handling the stress of pressure to perform. Brenda had difficulty asserting her views, especially when her ideas or opinions were different from those of the other directors in the room. She often had great ideas to improve her company's success. They need only implement them.

Brenda's frustration stemmed from her perceived lack of ability to clearly state her original thinking on an issue. Imagining all the objections someone might have to her claims, she often trailed off or waited to speak until the moment passed. She adopted the strategy outlined above and found that by noticing her breathing, selecting a focus word (hers was ASSERT), and using the power statement "I know what I'm talking about," she learned to be more direct.

In our women's forum, Brenda practiced how to pitch one of her ideas to a large group. In the dry run, she presented an overview of why the company should initiate a new customer loyalty program. She made her case assertively and received great feedback from the group. When the time came to make the pitch for real, she felt confident to speak up. Brenda succeeded in getting her company's buy-in to launch a pilot program applying her idea. She reports that she continues to feel less pressure while expressing her ideas and getting support in implementing them.

 # Action D: Stay present and rehearse a positive outcome

All the action items discussed above help retrain your brain to better cope with pressure. This option goes even deeper yet. It embraces anxiety and helps you manage outcomes from the inside out.

Recently, I was reading *The Pressure Principle* by Dave Alred, performance coach to star athletes, specifically the chapter on anxiety. Later the same day, I read an article on Focusing by David Rome in Tricycle Magazine, a Buddhist publication.

I love when information from diverse sources converges. Let me explain. What connected for me in reading both pieces was that the authors recommended allowing ourselves to feel anxiety, and then reframing that feeling to improve performance and growth. In my work, I regularly see how pervasive high anxiety is in business, and how society trains us to view anxiety as a negative. The main message we receive from peers, the media, and cultural norms in general is to try to ignore anxiety, medicate it with alcohol or pills, or see a therapist about it. Of course, the latter can help with chronic severe anxiety, but some degree of this emotion is a normal part of life. Both authors argued that feeling anxiety can be a good thing. I agree.

Alred builds a case for reframing anxiety by describing it as fuel to enhance performance. He discusses how athletes often ignore strategic plays in sports if the stakes are high, and instead choose ones that have a better probability of moderate success, resulting in mediocre performance. He attributes this avoidance behavior to the athlete's need to reduce anxiety and play it safe. Rome discusses how meditation trains us to detach from anxiety and stay present in cases where doing so can benefit us. He makes a distinction between meditation as a way of detaching from emotions and letting them float by and "focusing" as a way to be with our emotions so that we don't avoid them. He defines "focusing" as welcoming uncomfortable feelings and sitting with them to bear witness. By doing so, you allow the anxiety to subside, and you have the opportunity to transmute anxious feelings into more confident ones.

We have all developed clever ways to skirt anxious feelings. Are any of these yours?

- Switching on Netflix or a sporting event.
- Eating another piece of key lime pie.
- Having a cocktail to decompress.

Before you escape, consider staying present with your feelings of anxiety in a quiet setting. Breathe regularly and stay with the feelings, let go of what you are thinking or telling yourself. Notice the intensity of your anxiety dissipating. Relax into that space. When you are ready, picture yourself performing the task or doing what you most want to avoid while in a positive frame.

- See the golf shot land on the green.
- Picture yourself speaking in an engaging way as you address a group.
- Feel confidence as you hold a difficult conversation with a colleague.

Positive rehearsal of your preferred outcome takes hold when you stabilize anxiety and open yourself to new energy. You increase the chances for your preferred result because you set yourself up for a positive outcome. Countless studies of athletes and others who mentally practice desired results (such as hitting the ball over the net or putting it into the hole) show that mental practice is as effective as physical practice. Practice anyone?

 ## Action E: Decide now how to overcome obstacles

All of us feel the sting of rejection. Perhaps you didn't get into the college of your choice, get a date with someone you had a crush on, or receive a promotion. Failure to achieve a treasured goal makes it more difficult to adopt and sustain a positive attitude. The experience of failing at something we really want despite our effort and positive thinking is disappointing. Our culture tells us "think big," "don't give up," and "follow your heart." Do we focus so much on keeping a positive attitude that we miss internalizing our part in not achieving the goal or dream?

Case study: Megan

Megan did all she could to achieve her dream of becoming a division director for a large firm. "I pictured what it would look like. I followed a development plan that my boss and I had worked on to get me there. I received positive feedback in the interviews…yet I still managed to not get selected," she said. Recent research on positive thinking suggests that her entirely positive approach pushed the opportunity away.

Featured on National Public Radio's program Hidden Brain, researcher Gabriele Oettingen states that positive thinking and visualizing achieving our goals may not be the best advice. Her book *Rethinking Positive Thinking* challenges conventional wisdom about goal attainment. Oettingen found that "positive fantasies make you feel accomplished and take the energy away," meaning that the brain thinks it's already accomplished the goal, and the energy to achieve it dissipates. Studies conducted by Oettingen show that simply imagining a positive outcome produces lackluster results in comparison to a technique of "mental contrasting," in which subjects think about both the outcome they want and the setbacks that could stand in their way.

The steps in Oettingen's mental contrasting approach follow the acronym WOOP. First, identify your highest wish (W).

Second, target the outcome you desire (O). Then ask, "What is the inner obstacle that stands in the way?" Oettingen stresses that, when you internalize the role you might play in blocking the achievement of your goal, you enhance the chances of success.

Third, identify your "inner obstacle" (O) and state to yourself, "If that obstacle occurs, then I will _____." Fill in the blank with the behavior you will work on that may be impeding your progress.

Fourth, plan (P). As you move toward your goal, you strengthen your chances to achieve it by taking responsibility for your part in creating an obstacle. The last step of the WOOP model is to plan (P) your next steps to achieve your goal.

To extend the example, if Megan used the WOOP approach, she would have discovered a behavior that was sabotaging her success. Megan, like many high achievers, suffers from "imposter syndrome." In the syndrome, despite outward success, a person doesn't feel adequate. She doubts herself and internally feels like a fraud. Leaving this internal block unaddressed could have affected Megan's confidence and been a factor in her missing the opportunity. For instance, refraining from seeking feedback on new ideas because she feared that sharing plans that weren't fully thought out would expose her as incompetent. (Learn more about imposter syndrome in Chapter 1.) With a plan in place to tackle this behavior, her chances for the promotion improve.

Whatever your internal block is, ask yourself if you are impeding your own progress toward a long-desired goal because you are not self-aware. Discovering your own blocks can come from journaling, feedback from others, or taking time to get in touch with feelings you might be masking in the busyness of the day. A modern-day office may look like a calm and safe environment. However, it takes tremendous courage to perform well especially when you are scared. This holds true for professional women—but this type of courage is accessible.

 ## Seizing Success: Lorain's Story

Sergeant Lorain Prevaux served in the Iraq war under General Norman Schwarzkopf, Jr. When the general retired, Lorain was one of two people invited to address him in an event held in Tampa's Raymond James Stadium and broadcast around the world.

Terrified, she admitted that none of her close encounters in the military created as much stress for her as the assignment to thank the general in one single minute. Yet she rose to the occasion, saying (in part) "Your courage showed us how to be courageous. Your integrity inspired ours. You are our commander, our hero, and our friend; when we stand and salute you, we are not only saluting the uniform, but the very special man who wears it."

Schwarzkopf's eyes filled with tears, and after Lorain stepped from the platform he ignored military protocol and embraced her.

Despite the magnitude of this assignment and its importance to her, Lorain had a significant advantage as compared to many women who experience expectation anxiety. Her pressure revolved around a very specific, stand-alone task. As such, she focused all her energy on a single moment at a specific time. The expectations were clear; her audience was well-defined.

On a day-to-day basis, women face far more complex and intertwined challenges. We face often-conflicting expectations, some of them internally generated that have the potential to create a situation in which it feels like we just can't win.

 ## Review the five growth strategies in this chapter

There is no quick fix to handling performance pressure. See if any of these five effective strategies can make a difference in your life:

A. Embrace what you fear and make it a game.
B. Recall a past success.
C. Breathe and find the right word.

D. Stay present and rehearse a positive outcome.
E. Decide now how you will overcome obstacles.

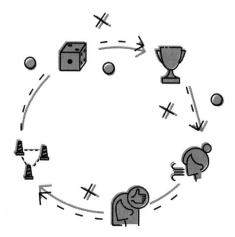

The more clarity you create about what is really expected, the better able you will be to channel your energies and produce results that make you proud.

Just as Lorain could not remove the pressures she felt, you will not be able to deliver on ambitious goals without feeling the heat. That means not just facing your challenges, but being honest with yourself about why you find them so challenging.

Take Action: Experiment and consider these questions:

When facing a fear or obstacle, I recommend that you ask yourself five questions:

1. How do I define success?
2. What are the things I'm avoiding right now that impede my success in the long term?
3. If I could be assured of success for myself, what would I see?
4. How can I create a habit where I expose myself to something I fear without taking it so seriously?
5. How can I practice the things that really count on a regular basis?

The more specific you are about what "success" means, the better you can separate unrealistic, overly perfectionist goals from the really important ones—the ones that allow you to play large and exceed expectations in a sustainable way.

Success is not being perfect. It is not being all things to all people, or making a situation okay for everyone else. As you develop your own definition, you start to set reasonable expectations for yourself, feel less compelled to make everyone happy, and even celebrate your successes.

The feedback you receive from this experimentation can create a breakthrough result for you. You may feel some short-term discomfort, but you enhance your chances of attaining a meaningful long-term goal by developing the habit of performing under pressure.

Don't mistake politeness
for lack of strength.

-

Sonya Sotomayor

Chapter 4:

Assertiveness — A Double-Edged Sword

Katy Mims was my friend and mentor—and next-door neighbor—for over 20 years. Katy was a fifth-generation Floridian who started out as a journalist, worked her way up to becoming a successful entrepreneur, and lived to the age of 100. I often walked over to Katy's to seek her guidance when I encountered challenges in my career, or sometimes just to have a glass of wine at the end of a long day.

One time, I sought her counsel for a difficult situation at work. No one in a client meeting seemed to hear my suggestion, but 15 minutes later when one of the men in the room said the same thing everyone responded enthusiastically. I had no idea how to handle this frustrating and awkward situation.

Katy took off her glasses, looked me in the eye and said, "Take heart—your suggestion was so good that someone took it forward. Next time, chime in and remind everyone that they heard the same thing before."

Katy affirmed my feelings. Her advice helped me wake up and see that I could respond differently and more directly with others instead of stewing over not feeling heard by my co-workers. She taught me to become more assertive and resilient— qualities that she, a true "steel magnolia," had in abundance. Katy called this sort of determination "gumption."

We need gumption. Almost every time I facilitate one of our Key Women's Leadership Forums, I hear at least one story from a woman who—like me in the story I told about Katy—let others talk over her without asserting herself. Maybe she didn't claim credit for her great idea. Or she didn't ask for the raise, high-profile assignment, or board exposure she wanted. Or she didn't voice her concerns about a risky decision her team was making because she feared being branded as disagreeable.

It amazes me how many bright, outwardly successful women don't ask for what they want or need because they fear the consequences or are waiting to be noticed instead of speaking up. When we don't stick up for ourselves, there's rarely anyone else to do so—and our careers suffer as a result.

 ## What we know

Staying silent and waiting for our great contributions to be noticed isn't working. The solution isn't as simple as speaking up and copying the assertive men around us; gender bias exists. The traits associated with strong leadership such as decisiveness, assertiveness and taking charge too often align with our view of men. These same traits in women can become misaligned if stereotyped expectations are to be nice, friendly, socially skilled, and sensitive. Culturally, we tend to view women differently from the way we view men; assertive women sometimes seem aggressive or "bossy" where the very same behavior in a man would be seen as direct. Directness is a positive leadership trait, aggressiveness is not. Women sometimes hold back because they rightly fear being penalized for speaking up too bluntly.

In her book *Lean In*, Sheryl Sandberg discusses a study done at Harvard to prove that point about the mismatch in qualities between leadership and being a woman. In the "Heidi/Howard" study, Harvard professors asked students to read a case based on Heidi Roizen, a successful real-life entrepreneur. All of the MBA students read the case study about Roizen's career, but half were given a version of the case in which Heidi's name had been changed to Howard.

The professors then polled the students about their impressions of Heidi/Howard. The students rated the entrepreneur as competent in both cases. Both versions showed an entrepreneur with significant accomplishments. However, the students found Howard to be a more appealing colleague than Heidi. They saw Howard as someone you would want to work for or with, while Heidi was viewed by some as selfish and "not the type of person you'd want to hire or work for." Again, the only difference in the case studies was changing the sex of the first name.

In an episode of the BBC program *The Inquiry*, people going through gender transitions consistently stated that they experienced more gender bias as women than as men—whether they went from male to female or female to male. When physically appearing female, the participants reported not being heard in conversations or meetings as much, losing opportunities for promotion, and being offered lower compensation than their male counterparts for the same jobs. When people began presenting as male, the result was just the opposite—more respect, better compensation, more chance of being heard. It's clear that it's not simply a "feminine" leadership style that's holding women back.

Two researchers, Melissa Williams of the Wall Street Journal and Larissa Tiedens of Stanford's Graduate School of Business, were curious whether or not the same assertive behavior would be seen differently coming from a woman versus a man. They synthesized 71 studies that tested people's responses to men and women behaving assertively (Williams; Williams and Tiedens). The pair found women were disparaged more than men for the same assertive behaviors. Interestingly, women were criticized especially often for direct verbal forms of assertiveness, such as negotiating for a higher salary. The same behavior displayed by men didn't elicit a negative response. The researchers' conclusion is that female leaders definitely get penalized for being "too assertive."

There is no perfect solution for women dealing with implicit bias in the workplace. Many of the women I coach report having tried to avoid coming across as too assertive by spending time building relationships in the workplace. They might take staff to lunch regularly even when there's a backlog of projects due, or talk to staff often about their lives outside work.

Take Brenda, for example. Brenda shared with her forum members that she wanted to build rapport with her multi-generational team members who didn't always understand where the others were coming from. She initiated a variety of team building experiences that included off-sites. Jack, her boss, gave her feedback that she spent too much time on communication within her team. "We need solid results," Jack added. The ironic thing was that in this case, Brenda's team was on schedule to execute on time and on budget.

The strategy of stepping up relationship building can mitigate being labeled as aggressive, but there is a downside - being seen as spending too much time on the wrong things, even if it's only a perception not based in fact. If a woman decides that she wants to be nurturing to people, some may doubt her as a leader because they don't want her to be too soft. A stereotype still exists that women in leadership roles are more interested in being liked or taking care of people than in the bottom line. If behaving "like a man" and behaving differently from a man both come with dangers, women need to be even more skillful at being assertive.

We could use new framing

What does assertiveness really mean? Assertiveness is the ability to confidently stand up for yourself, others, or your ideas in a non-aggressive, calm, and direct way. It's asking for what you need or want and letting the other party know why—no excuses necessary.

Effective assertiveness is both verbal and non-verbal communication. Non-verbally, assertiveness involves physical posture, direct eye contact, voice tone, pitch, and appropriate gestures. For example, if you ask to be considered for a coveted assignment, are you looking your manager in the eye, standing or sitting tall, and speaking in a clear tone? Or are you looking down, fidgeting, and hard to hear?

It's not that women don't know we're supposed to be assertive, or don't try. Although when we do ask for that raise or promote that great idea, we're often nervous or conflicted and wind up sounding tentative. When our tone is tentative, we don't get the results we want.

Furthermore, effective assertiveness requires going through an internal process to reflect on the very questions that can be our obstacles, such as:

- Why is it when I speak up no one seems to hear me?
- Why do I have to be nice all the time?
- Why is it when I'm direct people sometimes see me as a "bitch"?

Our internal dialogue keeps us from being effective in our assertiveness. Some women become tentative in how they assert and even wind up turning their assertion into a question. Others become strident and alienate the other party in their attempts. The first step is to become aware of what you are saying to yourself or thinking. Monitor your self-talk and challenge the assumptions you might be making.

When you decide to be direct, how can you re-frame a strong reaction to your assertion differently so that you stay centered and confident? A key factor here is to be clear on what you are asserting and why it's important to do so. In other words, the meaning you attribute to why you spoke up or defended your strategy or asked for a pay raise helps you to internalize the reason your assertion is important, even critical. In that frame, a comment from your boss or a peer would have less weight since you are coming from a place of clarity and can re-frame how you interpret their responses. Like confidence, effective assertion is an internal process, not just an external one.

While asserting, it's important to be clear about your intention and what you'd like to request or say. One of the most effective assertiveness strategies I use for myself and with clients is to use "I" statements vs. "you" statements. "I" statements show that you are taking ownership of your feelings and ideas and not placing blame. People can listen more openly when someone says "I feel frustrated when I don't understand what you're asking me" instead of "You are not communicating clearly." "I" statements invite conversation while "you" statements can make others defensive and shut down communication.

5 Strategies to Seize Success While Asserting

Here are five effective strategies to improving your assertiveness. As you read, see which appeal to you as an approach with which you can experiment.

Action A: Use powerful non-verbal assertiveness

In my coaching work on developing "executive presence" in others, I found non-verbal communication essential to leadership success.

How you attend to others non-verbally – using eye contact, staying present, and actively listening – all make a difference in how you are perceived. I've conducted organizational analyses where employees are interviewed about a leader's capabilities. Consistently, the leaders who use non-verbal communication most effectively are the ones singled out as "great" leaders. Comments like, "she made me feel like I was the most important thing on her calendar" or "he really cared about what I had to say" are the types of comments people make about leaders who understand the power of non-verbal communication.

One of the findings from Melissa Williams and Larissa Tiedens is that only verbal assertiveness penalizes women, not non-verbal assertive behavior. The researchers recommend that women use their bodies more consciously by doing things like taking expansive physical stances, narrowing the physical proximity between themselves and another person, and making direct eye contact. Furthermore, they state that "para-verbal" behaviors such as speaking loudly, targeting pitch and pace, and interrupting are also useful strategies, since they don't register as aggressive.

In her book *Presence*, Amy Cuddy outlines research showing the impact of physical presence on confidence and mindset. She and her colleagues found that using expansive body poses—like the "V for victory" body stance that winning athletes take when they cross the finish line of a race—impact testosterone and cortisol levels in both women and men. She reports that powerful leaders have high levels of testosterone and low levels of cortisol. High cortisol levels are associated with high stress. She points out that this balance between high testosterone and low cortisol plays out in the animal kingdom as well with alpha animals; the combination is typical of a powerful leader.

You can change your physiology by taking on large and confident stances to fill up the space around you. Changing your body changes your thinking. Cuddy discussed experiments she conducted showing that holding certain poses for two minutes before an interview positively affected how people performed in stressful job interviews. Not only did the people who held power poses do better than the control group, but those taking small and weak stances before the interviews did more poorly. It's no surprise that naturally confident people have confident body language, but even feigning confidence can help you tap into that power.

The main take-away from Cuddy's work is that our minds change our bodies and our bodies change our minds, all potentially resulting in better outcomes. "Fake it until you make it"—it really works. Two of the most effective power poses are:

1. "Starfish," in which you stand tall, legs apart and arms in the air in a V, and
2. "Wonder Woman," in which you stand tall with legs apart and hands on your hips.

Hold each pose for 2 minutes before a high-stakes situation and it positively impacts your confidence and your assertiveness.

 ## Action B: Monitor and change your internal dialogue

Accept your feelings as you are challenged and realize that "this too shall pass." It's easy to get stuck in a negative feeling and think, "Will it always be this way?" Negative self-talk and "awfulizing" a situation can keep you stuck. Notice what you are saying to yourself and alter it with a positive. For example, instead of thinking "I can't possibly endure any more", substitute that self-talk with "I'm looking at this as a challenge and am confident that I will get through it."

As humans, the old portion of our brains still influences how we feel, our internal dialogue or self-talk, and how we ultimately behave. The fear generated to protect us resulting in our "fight or flight" tendencies is the same fear that generates the self-talk that keeps us from growing. We wind up staying stuck in a protective mindset.

The first step is to become aware of what you are saying to yourself or thinking. Monitor your self-talk and challenge the assumptions you might be making. Are your assumptions related to learning and growing or do they fall more in the "protect myself and what I know" camp? Our inner dialogue shapes our mindset and attitude, positively or negatively. If you have a negative inner critic, challenge it and replace negative self-talk with a positive affirmation. For example:

Inner critic: "I won't bother with asking for that pay raise. My boss will say no anyway."

Affirmative supporter: "The scope of my work has expanded and I'm responsible for more projects than ever. I deserve to be compensated more since I'm doing the work of two people."

Inner critic: "That won't matter. Besides, it's been hard for others to appreciate all I do."

Affirmative supporter: "I will take some time to think through why I deserve a raise and build the rationale to get it."

The antidote is to rise above our demons and monitor what we say to ourselves from a more detached perspective. As difficult as this detachment can be to achieve, it affords us the chance to change our self-talk. Then we consciously choose the mindset we need to affirm success. It's from this perspective that we really help ourselves and others as well as see options that we would surely miss if we let our old brains rule.

Action C: Be graceful, but AFFIRM, ASSERT, AND AIM

Co-founder of BET, Sheila Johnson is the first black female billionaire. BET sold to Viacom for $3 billion in 2002. Johnson currently serves as Founder and CEO of Salamander Hotels & Resorts. Johnson recently spoke at an event where she received an award. Her advice for the women attending was clear and concise: "We don't use our own power enough—we should. Use it gracefully, but use it."

Johnson commented on a pattern of lack of assertiveness that she has observed in women, exacerbated by some of the barriers even successful women like Johnson experience in a male-dominated business culture. "[Women] just aren't in the conversation. When we fight to try to do that, we're called the 'B' word, even when we try to advocate for ourselves. Men watch out for themselves. Women do not do that" (Manning).

Despite Johnson's phenomenal success, she has never been asked to serve on a corporate board. So many of the executive women I coach aspire to serve on boards. It's depressing to learn that even Johnson doesn't get asked.

Even when you have "made it" financially, you need to assert yourself when dealing with business negotiations, advises Johnson. She learned the landscape over time, "Men use other people's money. Women usually don't get the same opportunity." Johnson has been cut out of some big deals even though she was in a position to play. The last time she wasn't invited into a deal, she pivoted and aimed higher. She put together a group of women who each invested $1M, and they launched WE Capital. WE's mission is "to advocate and invest in female leadership with the dual aim of promoting social impact and generating financial returns." WE is on its way to great success and benefits for those involved.

So, what are the lessons learned from Sheila Johnson?

First, you need to AFFIRM. The internal process of affirming that "this is what I really want" brings clarity and intention to the situation or goal.

Secondly, ASSERT your view, why it's important, and how it could benefit others and not just yourself. Formulate what you are going to say and rehearse. Women have more of a tendency to think or hope that they will be offered opportunities based on their competence and hard work. Waiting to be noticed is not a good strategy. As Johnson has suggested, you can do it gracefully, but do it.

Lastly, AIM for what you want, and if you can't find the right network leap and start your own. For example, if you want to connect with women in marketing and your local association isn't a good fit for you, organize an invitation-only event to bring together women in marketing whom you respect and can learn from. Create the kind of network you want, and make it an ongoing group with a unique focus.

 ## Action D: Say NO without the guilt

Some women are able to say "no" to a request or opportunity and feel good about it. "This isn't the right fit for me" or "I don't have the bandwidth right now—I hope you understand" are ways they opt out confidently. Others avoid saying "no" altogether because they don't want to jeopardize a relationship or disappoint the asker. They may say "yes" and pretend all is well, even though they are feeling stretched thin, bad about the situation or even resentful toward the requester. This is where classic passive-aggressive behavior takes root.

Then there are those in between, who ponder whether they should fulfill a request or take on an added responsibility. They spend time weighing what they might do and doubt sets in. They say "no" in as respectful a way as they know how: "I can't take this on right now" or "I'm sorry, I don't have the time" are frequent replies. Upon saying "no," there's a moment of relief. Then, for many, guilt arises. The resulting rumination is as bad as taking on the request. Herein lies the conundrum of "when I say no, I feel guilty."

So, what can we do to avoid the consternation and wasted time spent on guilt or regret? There are several steps you can take to address the aftereffect of saying "no." The first involves finding clarity on *why* you want to say no. Have you thought the request through? How does the request support your priorities and goals or those of people you care about? Is this the best time to decide, or are you currently tired or feeling overwhelmed?

If you lack clarity in the moment, give yourself time. Tell the person that you would like to consider their request and get back to them. Often, we feel pressure to say yes or no on the spot. Take that pressure off yourself.

If you decide your answer to the request is no, think about how you can respectfully communicate that without over-explaining. My dear friend and mentor Katy had one of the best responses for this situation, one that I've used successfully many times. She recommended saying "Thank you so much for thinking of me (or for the opportunity). I'm going to pass right now. I appreciate your asking." The underlying principle is to be kind and brief. No need to give excuses.

What happens next? Imagine that you've asserted yourself as described above, but now you feel guilty. You can't stop replaying the situation in your mind. You start ruminating about what happened and put valuable energy into regretting what occurred. Dwelling on the past turns into a habit, a mental groove, or mindset that becomes automatic; you stop thinking productively and start focusing on things that you can't change.

A useful strategy here is to acknowledge your feelings of discomfort, regret, or guilt. Next, find an affirmation that resonates with you like "It's important for me to honor my decision to say no," or "Saying no opens me up to other options."

Catch yourself when you start to go back to the past. Stay in the here and now. Get in touch with your body by noticing your breathing or taking some deep breaths; this can help bring you back to the moment. Some people develop a cue. When they are in the present, they might squeeze their index finger or tap their elbow. By pairing the feeling of staying present with a physical anchor, you can snap yourself out of those "what-if," "should-have" thought patterns.

Action E: Say NO when someone continues to insist

What happens if you find yourself challenged by the requester to give in? Some people persist and try to talk you out of saying no. One assertive approach to coping with this is called "fogging." Fogging involves agreeing with critical truths the requester presents and still doing what you want: saying no.

For example, you say no respectfully to the request to head the United Way campaign at work because you have too many work projects and commitments to your family, and because you've done it before. Your requester continues to talk about the good work the charity will do under your leadership. To apply fogging, you would say something like: "Thank you for your confidence in me. You're right, this organization does great work. I need to decline at this time." Continue to acknowledge the part that you agree with: "You're right, this organization does great work," and continue to decline.

What should you do if the person won't take "no" for an answer? Another assertiveness skill, "broken record," works best when the requester becomes more aggressive. It involves refusing to be deterred by anything the other person may say and sticking to your stance. The strategy with broken record is to keep saying in a calm, repetitive voice, "no," and why you can't or won't. In other words, repeat your original statement as the requester attempts to get you off track.

Ellen is the senior vice president of marketing for a technology company and participates in our Key Women's Leadership Forum. Her boss, the CEO, asked Ellen to fire an employee who reported directly to her. When Ellen asked why, The CEO commented that "she didn't listen well and for someone in that role, she should." Ellen felt this employee was doing a very good job—she was great to work with, met or exceeded her goals, and received rave reviews from both internal and external customers. Apparently, the CEO had one interaction with this employee that didn't go well. The employee is the company's meeting planner and was in the middle of a work crisis concerning the delivery of food for a big banquet. When she was distracted and appeared not to be listening to the CEO, he felt insulted. Ellen thought the CEO was being unreasonable and let his ego get in the way. She was surprised at how insistent he was about letting this employee go.

Ellen brought this issue up in the forum. She wanted to continue developing this person because she saw her talent and contribution. She felt her boss was criticizing the employee without any real data. Ellen adopted "broken record" and formulated the following response to his persistent urging to fire the meeting planner: "I appreciate your feedback. Right now, I'd like to coach this person first before taking any extreme steps." She continued to repeat this statement until the CEO acquiesced. Ellen took a risk because letting the employee go would have compromised her values—she believes in coaching and developing others. Over time, the CEO began to see that this employee was an asset to the company and seemed to let go of his initial judgment.

 ## Seizing Success: Susan's Story

If challenged by the person you are attempting to assert yourself with, hear them out, ask questions to make sure you understand where they are coming from, and, if warranted, give them credit for the part with which you agree. It's important not to get defensive. Stick to the facts throughout the interaction. Think about how the course of action that you are proposing might be a "win-win" for all concerned. Modifying your original request is part of the win-win process—just don't give up when what you are asserting is important to you and others.

An example of thinking through how your assertion can be a win-win is Susan. She is a VP of Operations at a large entrepreneurial, privately–held company and reports to the CEO.

They enjoy a good working relationship and Susan is passionate about what she does.

A year and a half ago, the CEO promised Susan that she would become part of the company executive profit-sharing plan, as all the others reporting to him already have (all men). Susan waited patiently. She finally decided to have a conversation with her boss to remind him of his promise. The conversation was hurried and the CEO seemed distracted. He indicated that he was planning to offer her the options "soon."

Susan brought this issue to our forum for discussion and advice. A big question for Susan was how and when to be assertive about being the only executive team member without the profit-sharing plans. The forum members asked some great questions that got Susan thinking. Here's a sampling:

- When you look at what is important to you in your career, how does this opportunity stack up?

- What is your strategy now that you've gone back and received assurance you will get the profit-sharing plan?

- Tell us more about the CEO and what his communication style is like. When you've been successful in influencing him in the past, what did you say/do?

The strategy many of the forum members suggested was to approach the CEO again in a more intentional way. Through a role play, we rehearsed how Susan could assertively address the situation with the CEO, understand his position better and create urgency for him to follow through. Susan left the meeting feeling more prepared and clearer about what she wanted to say, questions she would ask and how to present herself assertively.

Susan suggested a time to meet with her boss towards the end of the day when he might feel less distracted. She stayed calm and firm in her request. Susan started by reviewing the past times the two of them had discussed profit sharing and what her understanding was. She took the risk to ask if he had any hesitations. The CEO shared that he had been working on a "big deal" and although her compensation package was important, he did back burner it temporarily.

Susan re-asserted her expectations in a direct and factual way. She asked for a specific timeframe. Her assertiveness alerted the CEO that her request needed to become a higher priority. He wound up getting the process started by involving the CFO in putting together a package for Susan.

Review the five growth strategies in this chapter

You reviewed five viable strategies that can improve your assertiveness and minimize some of the gender bias that exists for women. When you feel reluctant to speak up, you can:

> **A. Use powerful non-verbal assertiveness**
> **B. Monitor and change your internal dialogue**
> **C. Be graceful, but AFFIRM, ASSERT AND AIM**
> **D. Say NO without the guilt**
> **E. Say NO when someone continues to insist**

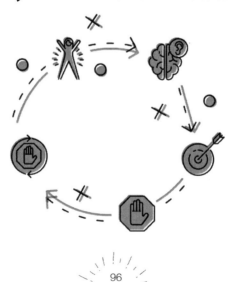

You are not limited to one of these strategies. Try them all depending on the situations that arise in your work and life. Assertiveness is essential to your self-respect, well-being, and happiness. It's also critical when you are in a leadership position and you are asserting for others.

Assertiveness shouldn't happen in isolation. You also need to take into consideration the context of the situation.

- Who are you speaking with?
- What is their frame of reference?
- Is the timing right to bring up this topic?
- How do they think/feel about the situation?
- What are some possible win-wins?

Be clear on your intention and for what you are asking. Rehearse your approach and get feedback from others so that you can try out different ways of communicating directly. Practice your non-verbals and consider using some confidence-building body stances ahead of a high-stakes interaction.

Take Action: Experiment and consider these questions

Think about the various ongoing situations you face at work and at home where you haven't felt heard or appreciated and ask yourself these questions:

1. How do I feel and why? What is my body telling me?
2. Am I standing up for what I think is right, or right for me? Why or why not?
3. What is important for me to say in this situation?
4. How can I rehearse being assertive and get good feedback?
5. How can I create a habit of saying no graciously, but firmly when I don't want to accept a request from someone?

Answers to these questions help you to analyze when and how to assert yourself constructively. Like all actions that produce results in life, being assertive is about taking a risk. It means letting go of old learning and picking up new ways of communicating directly when it counts.

Reacting in anger or annoyance will not
advance one's ability to persuade.

-

Ruth Bader Ginsburg

Chapter 5:

Influence — A Key to Leadership Success

A headhunter approached Jennifer, the vice president of marketing at a financial services firm, and enticed her into applying for a new position as head of product marketing with a fast-growing company. As she went through the selection process and interviewed with the company, she became more and more attracted to the opportunity. She liked the culture of the company as far as she could read it, the person who was to be her manager, and the role she'd play in the company as outlined.

Jen, as her friends call her, felt undervalued in her current role, though she enjoyed the marketing work she did and the people she led. She tried on several occasions to boost her compensation with little success. Typically, she tried waiting until she had built up a long track record of successes and she believed her value was already evident to her supervisor. Then she'd bring up the topic of a raise by presenting graphs and figures to prove that the marketing efforts she'd led had been successful. In return, she heard that her efforts were appreciated, but her compensation was already in line with industry norms and there wasn't money in the budget for anything more. This time, Jen determined she would get what she felt was fair compensation and perks, like more vacation time.

They selected Jen as the top candidate for the position. She reviewed compensation data on what positions like this new one typically pay in the Southeast, where she lived. Jen took time to outline a strategy on how she would negotiate her package. Despite her preparation, she felt unsure about how to influence her soon-to-be new boss. Her unsuccessful attempts to improve her compensation package in the past kept crossing her mind.

 ## What we know

One of the areas where women lag behind men is in pay. For every dollar that a man makes, a woman makes 79 cents. There are many reasons for this discrepancy, from female-dominated industries paying less, to women being penalized for taking time off to care for young children. But one that gets mentioned over and over is that women don't negotiate as well as men, or at all, when offered a position. According to a 2016 Glassdoor survey, 68% of women taking a new job accepted the pay they were first offered, compared to 52% of men ("3 in 5 Employees Did Not Negotiate Salary"). The confidence and ability to influence an employer to compensate you fairly is an important issue for women.

Whether you position yourself for higher pay in a new position like Jen, engage others to participate in a customer service initiative, or attempt to convince your spouse that you'd like to buy a new home, influence is at the core of our daily interactions—so much so that we don't often think about who we want to influence and why. Conscious awareness of what's important to the person we want to influence, and the best way to do that ethically, makes a big difference in the results we get at work and in life.

One tactic people fall back on is the old model of deferring to authority—in other words, trusting the judgment of the decision-maker and showing faith that they'll do the right thing. We think this will ultimately work in our favor because it shows respect for someone we want to win over. It has one other big advantage—it doesn't require us to do as much. In Jen's case, proving herself on the job and trusting her boss to see that she was worth it didn't require her to step out of her comfort zone. After all, marketing was already her area of expertise; negotiation wasn't.

But this strategy doesn't work—not in the long run, and often not in the short. In the long run, using this technique leaves us feeling powerless. We want to feel like we have a choice and have some autonomy in pursuing challenging work or in decision-making.

In the short run, it can often backfire. The best time to ask for what you want is when you are negotiating to take a position. Men more often than women will negotiate their salary before coming on board; women less so because they hesitate and fail to take the risk, leaving opportunity on the table. A Harvard Kennedy School study found that unless a job listing explicitly states that pay is negotiable, men are *three times* more likely than women to initiate negotiation about how much they'll be paid (Liebbrandt, Andreas and List). In fact, women were also less likely to apply to jobs that didn't state salary was negotiable, suggesting women feel they need permission to ask for the pay they want. Clearly, this is one of the factors causing the pay imbalance between men and women.

Of course, women do often recognize the need to initiate a conversation and use negotiation techniques. However, when we do there's another pitfall that keeps us from being effective. Women and men who are untrained in a variety of negotiation styles often simply fall back on using persuasion techniques that work on *them*.

It's remarkable how the average person uses "their style" repeatedly to try to gain enthusiasm from someone who clearly has a different way to be influenced. For example, let's say you prefer a logical reasoning style and continue to use your preferred style to attempt to convince a co-worker to support a new product strategy. The "influencee," or the person you as the influencer want to persuade, may in this case prefer a style that is more consultative, where both of you explore the situation and seek information and opinions from each other. This type of influencee might feel uninterested or put off by having a series of logical points presented to them without being asked for their opinion.

As you learn which approaches people in your environment find most engaging and appropriate, you gain insight into what works and what doesn't. It's this step of learning from experience that many people are missing. They only know one or two styles of influence, and when those don't work, they conclude that it's hopeless or that it was presumptuous of them to ask.

What is influence? The movies portray persuasion as a matter of making a dramatic speech at the climax of the story (complete with music swelling in the background), or making a killer presentation that convinces everyone in the room they've underestimated you. It's more complex than that. Influencing is a critical competency of leadership effectiveness. It is the ability to impact others in such a way that they honor your request, take a course of action you recommend or make a change in how they behave or in their belief system. In essence, influence is getting others to take your lead.

However, influence is bi-lateral, meaning that when you attempt to influence someone else it's important to be open to their ideas and suggestions. You influence the other person and they in turn may influence you, so flexibility and looking for common ground are critical. For example, my friend Carol did her homework on what the car she wanted to buy should cost and was able to influence the salesman to meet her price. He then proceeded to show her upgrades in an attractive way, and she wound up spending $9,000 more than she planned.

Influencing is a skill, but it's not a simple skill that you can learn once and then keep deploying in the same way forever. It requires an adaptive mindset because you must consider the frame of reference and the needs of others to be effective at it. The situation and environment have to be right for the other person to say yes. The person you want to influence must also have the *ability* to say yes, and what you're asking or suggesting should not be in conflict with the other person's interests or values.

We could use new framing

What separates the best leaders from their less-effective counterparts is the ability to influence others, especially in challenging circumstances. How we frame things and how we present them have everything to do with whether or not we're successful in achieving our goal. A frame is a powerful way to show the relationship between something the other person values and your idea or suggested next step.

As with most progress in life, developing the skill of influencing starts with self-awareness. Are you aware of what influences you? How do others perceive you and the way you influence? Are you coming across in a way that aligns with your intent? In addition, the most successful influencers think ahead about what the other person's influencing style is and how to address it so they can better "frame" their stance.

There are many "styles" of negotiating. Does this person like facts and figures? Do they get inspired by a compelling vision? Do they like to barter? We tend to use the influencing style that we prefer to sway others, even though that might not be their preferred style. One of the biggest mistakes people make is not understanding the frame of reference of the person they want to influence and to come from their own instead.

I taught a program on Leadership & Influence at Stanford University for several years where 40 or so leaders from the hospitals and clinics area came together each year to focus on enhancing their leadership capabilities. All took a 360° assessment called the Survey of Influence

Effectiveness (SIE) that gives people a picture of how their boss, peers, direct reports, and others they work with view their use of influencing skills. Specifically, they get feedback on their strengths and where they can improve as it relates to influence. Furthermore, each participant becomes aware of their most frequently used influencing styles and how effective they are perceived to be by key people in their work environment.

Dr. Terry Bacon developed the assessment. He founded and built Lore International, a leadership development consulting firm that I partnered with in the past. (Lore has since been acquired by Korn Ferry, who now owns the SIE assessment.) So much of what I learned about influence over the years came from Dr. Bacon's work and the use of this assessment. Once people learn what their preferred style or styles of influencing are, they become more attuned to observing how others are influenced. Without awareness of one's own style and that of the person you want to influence, your chances of being successful are slim unless you both happen to have a similar style.

In the Stanford program, I used a real-world example featured on NPR that involved influencing doctors to join a rural clinic in Ashland, KS. As described in a 2012 NPR story by Peggy Lowe, Ashland, population 855, is a five-hour drive south of Kansas City. The Ashland clinic has 24 beds. The next-closest health center is 50 miles north in Dodge City, and the nearest Starbucks is 160 miles away (Lowe).

Benjamin Anderson was the clinic's CEO. He had a big challenge. The facilities were 55 years old, morale was low, and turnover was high. At the time, the clinic was without an administrator for 6 months and without a doctor for about 8 months. If the medical clinic closed down, Ashland would lose its school. When a community loses its school, it becomes a ghost town. In order to attract doctors to Ashland's clinic, Anderson knew he had to offer something different.

If Anderson tried to go after the general pool of doctors seeking jobs, his only option would have been to offer a big salary and rich benefits to counteract the perceived downsides of the position. The clinic couldn't afford all of that. Anderson's strategy was simple yet ingenious. He appealed to doctors whose values reflected a desire to go to remote areas and help others through medicine. He offered potential doctor candidates 8 weeks off to do missionary work in whatever country they chose. The rationale here is that if a doctor is willing to sleep on a cot in the Amazon or Haiti, he or she would be willing to serve in rural Kansas. Anderson calls it "mission-focused medicine." By appealing to the values of a very specific target group, Ashland found doctors who were mission-focused and weren't deterred by feeling isolated.

My firm offers programs on strategic influence. We recently delivered one to women who work in capital markets for a large financial services firm. The women participating often commented on how thinking about "my style" and what the other person's is made all the difference in their preparation to influence others.

5 Strategies to Seize Success While Influencing Others

Here are five effective strategies to improve or enhance your ability to influence. As you read, see which appeal to you as approaches with which you can experiment.

Action A: Be aware of your influencing style and that of the others

What are these "styles of influencing" I referred to earlier? In his extensive research on influence and power, Dr. Bacon targeted ten types of influencing styles (Bacon, *The Art of Influence*):

Legitimizing

A person using this influencing style often refers to authority or a higher body of laws, rules, procedures, customs, or traditions. The statement "We've always done it that way" is an example of legitimizing. People also legitimize by referring to recognized authorities such as a senator, police officer, professor, executive, or someone else whose opinion the person to be influenced respects. In the case of a salary negotiation, pointing to median salaries for people in your industry to show that you're getting paid less than the norm is an example.

Logical Persuading

As the name suggests, this means using logic to persuade others. This technique often involves data, graphs, evidence, and documentation. For instance, someone who wants to increase their annual budget makes a case for the bump up by showing last year's return on investment and how with added dollars, they can do even better this year.

Appealing to Relationship

Legitimizing and logical persuading are ways of explaining what you want. Appealing to relationship is a way of asking for what you want, and it means asking colleagues for favors or assistance. This is a powerful technique because colleagues are inclined to say yes to one another. An example would be when a co-worker asks you to cover for them while they take a three-week vacation.

Socializing

This technique is similar to appealing to relationship, except that you don't have an existing close relationship with the person you want to influence. When you socialize, you establish rapport with a person, find commonalities, and build a connection. People are more likely to be influenced by you if they feel a bond, however slight. Think of the person you meet at a fundraiser who identifies some of the things you have in common, like your kids both playing soccer or a mutual interest in running. When you see this person in the future you have a base to connect with each other.

Consulting

Another way of influencing is to invite the person to be influenced to participate in solving the problem, addressing the issue and finding a solution. You consult when you present a problem or issue and ask good questions soliciting the "influencee's" input. If you incorporate the person's suggestions, you create a collaborative solution the person to be influenced is more likely to support. Let's say you've been asked to lead a cross-functional team in your company to enhance quality in your line of products. Instead of crafting your own plan, you consult with the key people currently involved in making the products and get their input and ideas about how quality can be enhanced before initiating next steps.

Stating

The opposite of asking is stating, which means boldly and directly articulating what you want. If you state your position assertively and self-confidently, you are likely to influence a number of people. One of the strategies in the assertiveness chapter of this book perfectly aligns with this style of influencing. For example, when under consideration for a new position you boldly state that "I think I'm the right person for this position. Let me tell you why...."

Appealing to Values

This is one way to inspire others. You appeal to their values by showing how your request is important or how it is consistent with what they consider uplifting, exciting, or morally right. Appealing to values is an emotional approach that can attract people who look to align their values with what is being proposed. An example here is the 2018 Golden Globes, when Oprah accepted the Cecil B. DeMille award for outstanding contributions to the world of entertainment.

She was the first woman and first minority to receive this honor and gave an electrifying acceptance speech. Oprah appealed to the values of many women and men in the audience, encouraging them to not give up fighting for equality, and predicting that women will "become the leaders who take us to the time when nobody ever has to say 'Me too' again" (Friedman). Oprah encouraged others to see her award not just as a career success for her, but as a step toward equality in which other women, and victims of sexual violence involved in the #Metoo movement, could share.

Exchanging

This is formal or informal bargaining. When you exchange, you gain the cooperation of the person to be influenced by giving him or her something they value in exchange for something you want. Having a trusting relationship with this person is essential for effective exchange. An example might be your involvement in supporting a peer's recommended direction in the strategic planning process at your company. Suppose they have a favored candidate for a C-level position that will open up soon, while you want an increased budget for a special project you lead. If comfortable, you endorse their preferred job candidate in exchange for their support of your planning recommendations.

Modeling

Another way to inspire is to set the example, to model the behaviors you would like to see in others. Parents, coaches, teachers, counselors, and other leaders of all kinds use modeling as a way to influence others. Modeling is done over time, so it is a slower way to gain buy-in. Consistency is critical. For instance, if a teacher wants to encourage thoughtful discussion in class, they respond to student questions in the thoughtful and respectful tone they're hoping to foster. Think of a leader who influenced you positively. What were specific things they did and behaviors they modeled over time that made them important to your life and career?

Alliance Building

A "mega-style" of influencing involves building alliances of supporters who can help you influence others. This approach is collaborative and can be very successful; however, it takes time. Alliance-building involves several steps: identifying people who might want to ally with you, figuring out what their goals are and what they want that you can provide, and nurturing the relationships over time. For example, a woman leading a task force on gender diversity might recognize that she needs to include a strong group of people whom company leadership will be inclined to take seriously. She then identifies people in the organization who might be willing to devote time and energy to the project and considers each person's potential reasons for getting involved. These may include the task force inherently aligning with their values, their desire for recognition for their leadership abilities, their hope to strengthen their relationships with other task force members, or some combination of those factors. From there the task force conducts surveys and makes recommendations to the executive team on how the organization could implement more gender-friendly policies.

To identify your influencing style more specifically, visit Dr. Bacon's site at **http://www.theelementsofpower.com/index.cfm/ power-and-influence-self-assessments/** to take a free assessment.

Case Study: Values in Action

Back to Jen. Awareness of her style of influencing and that of her new manager was an important first step in her thinking through how she could earn the compensation she wanted. Jen noticed upon reflection that when she finally asked for compensation adjustments in the past, she liked using facts and figures to support her stance. Her new manager spoke a lot about the culture of the company and its core values in their conversations. She decided that she would be direct in her negotiating this time and ask for what she thought was fair, appealing to his values, using only facts and figures as a back-up.

In her final negotiation, Jen assertively stated what she wanted: "I appreciate your offer and am excited about contributing to the team and the company. You have a great culture here. For what you've outlined, the level of responsibility and the outcomes you expect, $X compensation with a 25% bonus opportunity is in line with the value I'd bring." Then Jen paused instead of rushing to facts and figures.

Jen got the position and felt great about the compensation she received. She realized that her focus on building a case wasn't the best strategy in this situation. Instead, she took time to think through the situation ahead and built up the courage to ask for what she wanted. She couched her request in a way her manager could hear her, and that made all the difference.

Action B: Be clear on your picture of success

What do you want to accomplish? Ask yourself: "If my highest wishes for an outcome were assured, what would happen?" or "What is the outcome I most desire?"

List what you'd like to see happen, and highlight those things that are "non-negotiable." I recently coached an entrepreneur who received an offer to sell her company to a larger one and become part of the leadership team. Her non-negotiable item was owning stock in the acquiring company from the start. Other aspects of the deal, such as price and the details of her role on the leadership team, were important but not as critical to her.

Here is a decision-making grid we've developed to assist people with getting clarity on what they really want when considering career options:

Career Criteria	Option 1	Option 2	Option 3
Independence – Being able to make my own schedule			
Compensation – Earning at least what I currently make and ideally 20-50% more			
Learning & Growth – Having the opportunity to go beyond my current skill set and expertise			
Purposeful Work – Engaging in meaningful work that plays to my strengths and is aligned with my passion			
Work Life Balance – Being able to balance work, home and personal desires while accomplishing the work at hand			
Achievement – Challenging myself and others to a new standard of excellence			

Rate each option against your career criteria on a 1-5 scale:
1 = does not meet criteria to 5 = meets all or most of the criteria

You can adapt this tool to the specifics of any decision-making situation before you decide how you want to influence and what your negotiables and non-negotiables are.

Action C: Be ready to listen so that you understand what can make it a win-win

Planning the questions you might ask as you enter negotiations with others is part of the preparation. It's easier to present what you want and trust that the other person will agree. By "telling," however, you miss the chance to learn more about what the other person values, their style of influencing, and their non-negotiables. You also run the risk of failing to influence the other party because you don't understand what's really important to them and don't have enough data to make it a win-win.

Take time to seek information and ask good questions. A good question in this context is one that is non-judgmental, open-ended, and delivered in the spirit of truly wanting to hear the other's view. Questions like:

- "Please explain the reason for your position?"
- "What is your picture of success for the outcome?"
- "What, if any, are your concerns about my proposal?"
- "What are the priorities you most want to focus on?"
- "Are there some other factors driving this that would be helpful for me to know that we haven't discussed?"

When possible, avoid questions answerable with a "yes/no" response or that require only small amounts of information. In negotiating, reciprocity often occurs naturally where you ask a question and then the other person asks theirs. If you use your turn in questioning on a poorly constructed or frivolous question, the other person may have an advantage if theirs is well thought out. Their question can take you on a different path than the one you anticipated and you may wind up talking a lot more than you thought you would. When negotiating, talking a lot is not usually a good thing. You don't want to reveal your weaknesses or let on that you'll accept less than you desire. Don't waste your time on questions that give little information and spur you into divulging more than you want or need to share.

Action D: Offer-Counteroffer

In his book *Never Split the Difference*, FBI hostage negotiator and business school lecturer Chris Voss outlines his theory on what works in influencing others, particularly in high-stakes situations. Voss states that rational problem-solving approaches to influencing others don't work unless you lay the groundwork through listening, trust-building, and empathy. These traditionally "soft skills" attract the emotional brain, which is where people typically start in the negotiation process, whether they are aware of it or not. The more rational part of influencing comes later, once the emotional brain is engaged.

Negotiating a price for services is an example for the rational part. Voss learned his recommendation for bargaining, called the Ackerman model (pp. 205-208), during kidnap-for-ransom situations. It may help you get a great deal. Here are the steps he outlines:

1. Set your goal or price.
2. Make your first offer 65% of your target price.
3. Have prepared three raises of increments; for example, 85%, 95% and 100% of your target price.
4. Use empathy, questions, and assertiveness to coax the other side to counteroffer before you increase yours.
5. When calculating your final amount, give the precise number, not the rounded version. For example, $21,798 vs. $22,000. The level of specificity it has adds credibility that resonates with people.
6. With your final offer, add in a non-monetary item that shows you are at your limit.

Voss has great success teaching others how to use the subtleties of influencing others around promotions, getting price reductions, and almost any other high-stakes situations. You can adapt this technique to a salary discussion. Professional salaries don't vary as wildly as ransoms paid to kidnappers, but you might lead with an offer that's 110% or 120% of the amount you want to get paid and then prepare to bargain down in increments. To show when you reach your limit and don't want to go any lower, offer to compromise on one of the non-monetary benefits you asked for, such as increased vacation time.

 ## Action E: Frame it for engagement

The power of conscious framing is probably one of the least-used and most effective skills that a leader employs. A frame is the set of assumptions and beliefs you have about a particular situation or task. Frames are a product of your past experiences and are neither good nor bad. The challenge or blind spot in this case is that we assume our framing reflects the truth instead of our own subjective view and we forget that others frame things differently.

For example, as a leader you might see a bigger vision for a new rebranding project and have a clear understanding about its importance to the organization. Those reporting to you might see the project as involving mundane tasks like revamping the website or reviewing advertisements. They may see a series of unreasonable deadlines with no clear end in sight.

You have a significant impact on how employees "frame" the project and, ultimately, on its success or failure. If someone frames the project as complicated and not really necessary they operate from that assumption. A leader's job is to create meaning for the individuals and the team participating in the project or initiative so that they frame the work as a stimulating challenge and see their contribution to it as important, even critical.

The topic of framing may seem insubstantial, but it has concrete effects. A study of technology implementations involving valve surgeries in cardiac surgery departments showed that the hospital teams who succeeded in adopting a new cardiac technology framed innovation differently than those who failed to implement the approach successfully (Edmondson).

Becoming skilled in the new surgery was a challenge because its less invasive nature made it harder for the surgical team to see what was happening and to insert small tubes and other implements. The more successful departments framed the new approach as a way for caregivers to fulfill their mission as healers by cutting down on patient pain and recovery time after surgery. They focused on "patient benefits and…on the desire to be a leading cardiac center" (Edmonson 42). By contrast, in the less successful departments, caregivers saw the change in approach simply as an inconvenience, or something they were ordered to do from the top down. This difference was the result of poor framing from head surgeons who relied on staff to simply "know their job" rather than communicating with them about the new procedure (39).

The difference between the most and least successful teams was striking: Two of the four hospitals discussed in the study completely abandoned the attempt to switch to the less invasive surgery. What's most instructive is that the researcher concludes that how leaders framed the project determined successful implementation, not management support, resources, project leader status, or expertise. Implementations framed consistently as learning opportunities with an important purpose did best.

As a leader, part of your job is to inspire others and help them see the relevance of what they are doing as it contributes to the bigger picture or vision. Here are some things to keep in mind while framing:

- See the project as an opportunity yourself and actively convey that to those involved.
- Let people on the team know that their role is essential to the project's success.
- Communicate often about the purpose and importance of the project and what you learn together.

No matter what your industry, framing is an essential tool for influencing that leads to leadership effectiveness and organizational success.

 ## Seizing Success: Sarah's Story

Sarah heads customer service for large insurance company. When I started coaching Sarah, she stated that her goal was to be more effective as a leader. When I asked her what that meant to her, she said, "I'd like to engage people to follow my lead more often." We drilled down further and identified that she would like to learn how to be "more convincing" as well as "inspiring" as a leader.

An important first step in coaching is to assess where the "coachee" is in relation to her goals. We conducted the Survey of Influence Effectiveness (SIE) survey described earlier. Sarah's boss, peers, direct reports, and clients completed the SIE 360 assessment in which Sarah received feedback on how effective she was as an influencer and which styles she used most. She also received feedback on her ability to inspire and engage others.

Sarah's feedback showed that her predominant style of influencing was to "appeal to values." She often referred to the values of the company and described how the course of action she proposed aligned with those of the company. Since serving customers was one of the company's core values, she often built her case around that value. Her backup style involved "consulting," as she worked effectively with others to brainstorm or resolve issues.

Some of the key people in Sarah's work environment reported that she could improve by being more analytical and logical in her approach at times. Her boss' predominant style was "logical persuading" and he sometimes found her approach "less than well thought out."

Sarah set her goal to improve identifying other people's styles and then adjust hers to enhance her ability to influence them. This includes testing out where they were coming from by observing them more closely and asking questions that elicit preferences, such as "Would you like to see the numbers on this?" or "Who else should we involve on this initiative?"

We developed a plan and personal success scorecard that guided Sarah in her leadership development goals. With effort and accountability, Sarah saw improvements in how she worked with her boss, her team, and others with whom she interacted. At the one-year mark, we re-administered the SIE. Sarah consistently rated higher over the previous year on the appropriateness, frequency, and effectiveness of her use of influencing styles. Comments included being "a model for other leaders in the company."

It's obvious that influencing others is central to success. We often think of the ability to win others over as mysterious—some charming quality or "art of persuasion" that is innate. Far from it. You can develop the skill of influence and reap the benefits of stronger allies and more successful negotiations.

 ## Review the five growth strategies in this chapter:

Here are five effective strategies to improving how you influence. As you read, see which appeal to you as an approach with which you can experiment.

> **A. Be aware of your influencing style and that of the others.**

B. Be clear on your picture of success.

C. Be ready to listen so that you understand what can make it a win-win.

D. Offer-counteroffer.

E. Frame it for engagement

Take Action: Experiment and consider these questions

Think about upcoming or ongoing situations at work or at home where influencing others is important to you. Ask yourself these questions to prepare:

1. What are my preferred styles of influencing?
2. Who do I want to influence in this situation and why?
3. What are my non-negotiables?
4. Who will be involved and what are their needs and desires?
5. What are some of the strategies I can employ to help make this a win-win or at least a fair compromise for all?

Answers to these questions help you think more strategically about how and when to influence. Like with all skills, practice builds your repertoire.

If you get, give. If you learn, teach.

-

Maya Angelou

Chapter 6:

Transformational Leadership - Inspiring Growth

Jessica had always been great with numbers. She made it into a top-tier business school, received her MBA, and was delighted to get a great job offer. Jessica felt that she was on her way to eventually achieving her big goal of obtaining a role as the CFO of a publicly traded company.

Fast forward several years, and that dream career wasn't working out. Jessica was in the same position, and she didn't feel like she was on the radar of the leaders at the company who made decisions about whom to put on the track towards the C-suite.

What went wrong? When I met with Jessica to explore her dilemma, I recognized the legacy of obstacles women in leadership face. One of the reasons Jessica failed to be tapped for a top leadership position is that, in her role as senior analyst, some colleagues found her to be too assertive and achievement-oriented. Jessica tried to "do leadership" in the way she saw modeled by the senior men around her. As research shows, the typical traits of male leaders—being assertive, authoritative, direct—are not usually viewed as attractive in women. Jessica displayed that behavior, and it backfired.

Jessica, while always respectful, frequently asserted her views and ideas on possible organizational and team improvements. In one incident six months after she was hired, Jessica proposed a new Enterprise Resource Planning (ERP) system to replace the company's outdated processes that impaired productivity. Her peers were less than enthused, believing that the effort in installing a new ERP wasn't worth the return at that time. There was also something about Jessica's approach that turned some of her co-workers off. One of her peers commented, "She just doesn't put it down. She continues to tell us how important something is and there's no buy-in." Performance reviews revealed that Jessica was perceived as competent, but not as "interpersonally skilled" or likeable as her peers.

Another obstacle Jessica faced was the difficulty of finding a workable balance between her professional and personal life. In the years since she joined the company, Jessica met her husband, Dan, and started a family. There were times when Jessica opted out of work-related requests, like taking an international assignment with lots of travel or working over the weekend on short-term projects, for family reasons. As many wives do, Jessica assumed the role of managing the household. At any given time, she knows what items the household is running low on and has a running mental calendar of cleaning tasks, errands and upcoming trips to the pediatrician. Dan helps out but is far more task-driven in his support of the household and childcare. Jessica is the manager of the household.

If you're married to or in a relationship with a man, this scenario might sound familiar to you. There's a reason for that. The 2017 Modern Family Index (Bright Horizons) showed that the role of all-around manager is twice as likely to fall on the shoulders of the woman in a partnership than the man (71% vs. 38%). The reality is even more unbalanced for parents, with 76% of moms versus 22% of dads keeping track of their children's schedules, pediatrician appointments, sports practices and science projects. With this perceived need to make sure nothing falls through the cracks, it's no wonder women are reluctant to embark on long business trips or sign on to weekend retreats. As Jessica learned, this commitment to family can be unfairly perceived as lack of commitment to work.

To Jessica's increasing frustration, she stopped receiving plum opportunities for advancement and development. She was no longer seen as possible successor to the CFO. As a result, Jessica began to miss out on the flow of power, referrals, and development opportunities more readily available to some of her male colleagues.

Women in leadership roles often step off the career fast track because of the excessive hours required. Even if you're single, don't have children or have a partner who pulls his or her full weight, the dynamic of women having higher household responsibility affects you. The commonness of this situation becomes a self-fulfilling prophecy. It reinforces the belief of people around you that you as a woman have less career commitment. On a psychological level, we combat against cognitive bias, a dynamic wherein people naturally notice behavior that supports their view, but not behavior that contradicts it. They perceive more stereotypical behavior than is really happening.

For example, the leadership at Jessica's company began to notice when she took time off or left early for family reasons, but they didn't notice when she stayed late to help her team or finish a project. Decades after women started fighting for complete career equality, old dynamics—like women missing out on opportunities because they're seen as too family-focused or can't join the good-old-boy network—are still very much a part of our lives.

Women bring unique strengths that can propel our careers and enhance our success in top leadership roles—if we manage to avoid certain pitfalls. Jessica's encounter with the mismatch between gender stereotypes and leader stereotypes is an example of one such pitfall. Her difficulty attaining an acceptable work/life balance is another.

When Jessica came to me for coaching, she was discouraged and wanted a change. She wasn't clear on what kind of a leader she wanted to be. One of the tools that I find most powerful for participants in leadership development programs I teach is for them to write what their leadership philosophy is and how they would like to see it implemented in their work and life. After much reflection, Jessica presented hers. She described her goal as inspiring others, engaging them to collaborate and creating meaning for herself and those she leads.

 ## What we know

Jessica's newly described philosophy excited me when I read it. Her words aligned well with a collaborative, meaning-driven style of leadership called transformational leadership that's evolved since introduced many years ago by political theorist James MacGregor Burns in his 1978 book *Leadership*. A transformational leader identifies needed change, creates a vision that guides others, and engages people in being part of something that is bigger than each individual job. In the process of working together, both the leader and team members achieve new levels of accomplishment. They grow together as they work toward a common vision and effect positive change.

A transformational leader builds relationships and rapport with followers over the long term. They create a sense of commitment by serving as a role model, connecting projects to the team member's values and inspiring a sense of collective identity. Think back to a boss, professor, sports coach or mentor with whom you loved working. Do any of these traits sound like them? That person probably made you feel like they were working with you to achieve something important, to you as well as to the company or team.

A transformational leader is authentic and engages and inspires people. Transformational leaders guide change through a compelling vision, building trust and confidence in those they lead and empowering them to develop their potential. A transformational leader knows that leading others effectively is about being willing to support the growth and transformation of others as well as their own. We talked in one of the chapters on Right Focus about clarifying your values and finding a career that's meaningful for you. As a leader, you can make that goal come true for those you work with, too.

Transformational leaders help people see the big picture and their part in it by asking: Where are we now in relation to that vision? What do we need to do to get there? What are the roles we can all play in making the vision reality? These leaders involve people in bridging the gaps and reinforcing the important part all play in the process. They focus on process as well as on outcome, so that every member gets a fair hearing and chance to contribute to decision-making and innovation.

Think back again to the leader who was most effective at inspiring you to work toward a goal, and you'll likely recognize most or all of these traits. Talking to Jessica, I saw that she had the desire and potential to become such a leader.

 ## We could use new framing

Transformational leadership has yet to become the norm in most company cultures. You've probably worked in a place where decisions were handed down from above, and workers were motivated solely through "incentives" and punishments. In the new paradigm of flattened organizations, more collaborative teamwork, and the need to work across time zones and international boundaries, it's more and more necessary to create a collaborative working environment.

If you want to be a transformational leader, you need good communication skills, a supportive attitude, willingness to put other's interests above your own, and ultimately the ability to build a base of trust with those you lead. These sound like the traits we often attribute to the female gender. Is it possible that women have a greater aptitude for transformational leadership?

The authors of the 2013 book *The Athena Doctrine* set out to examine the idea that "traditionally feminine values and traits were gaining in value and respect" (Gerzama and D'Antonio, 1). The results of surveys they conducted reveal that 57% of people worldwide were dissatisfied with the conduct of men in their country, including 79% of people in Japan and South Korea and over two thirds of Americans, Mexicans and UK residents. Among millennials, more than 80% express this dissatisfaction. These respondents believe "traditionally masculine thinking and behavior: codes of control, competition, aggression, and black-and-white thinking" are to blame for many current problems (4-5). Two thirds of survey participants (including more than half the men) agreed with the statement that "the world would be a better place if men thought more like women."

The book provides detailed insight into the gender traits people find desirable or damaging. Gerzema and D'Antonio presented respondents with a list of 125 different human characteristics and asked half the respondents to categorize them as masculine, feminine or neither. The other half were presented with the same words, but instead of being asked about gender, were asked to rate their importance to leadership, success, morality and happiness. Based on a survey of 64,000 people around the world, the results showed that the "feminine" traits made up 8 of the 10 traits deemed most important for leadership in today's world. The eight traits viewed as feminine are:

- Expressive
- Plans for the future
- Reasonable
- Loyal
- Flexible
- Patient
- Intuitive
- Collaborative

The two remaining traits seen as masculine are: Decisive and Resilient.

So, if there's a list of traits that cluster together as both "feminine" and desirable for leadership, what do they have in common? Consider the role of emotional intelligence (EI). Emotional intelligence is your capacity to recognize your own feelings and those of others and for you to manage your emotions effectively as well as for those you lead. When you are emotionally intelligent, you are aware of the impact you have on others. EI involves the behaviors that sustain people in challenging roles, or as their careers become more demanding. Two of the critical building blocks of EI are self-awareness and empathy.

Women are often more self-aware than men. This means women are more likely to perceive their own strengths and weaknesses accurately, track how others are reacting to them, and notice when they've made a mistake. A Hay Group study examined data from a 17,000-person database and found 19% of female versus 5% of male executives were rated as "perceptive in self-awareness" (Baldoni).

Women are also, on average, more empathetic as measured on some emotional intelligence assessments. They take time to listen and empathize with others. Empathy is the ability to capture the feeling and meaning of what another is experiencing and conveying it in such a way that the person feels understood. Emotionally, women are usually more attuned to what is going on. Arteche et al. (2008) gave detailed personality surveys to UK workers and found that females outscore males significantly on empathy, emotional skills, and emotional-related perceptions.

More recently, Meshkat and Najati similarly found that "females scored higher on emotional self-awareness, interpersonal relationships, self-regard, and empathy" (5). Women typically score high in tasks that involve perceiving emotion. They outperform men in recognizing facial expressions (Wingenbach, Ashwin and Brosnan). When presented with videos of faces displaying various emotions at low, medium and high intensity, the researchers found "a robust female advantage over males in recognizing a wide range of emotional expressions from videos" at all intensity levels. Have you ever been in a social setting and noticed that someone present seemed upset or was being left out of the conversation, while the men around you were oblivious to the problem? There's a reason for that!

This view finds support in the field of neuroscience. Meta-analysis of studies involving thousands of leaders suggests that women are more transformational in style than men. While many factors contribute to leadership performance—personality traits, values, motivations, training and experience, for example—scientific evidence confirms that men and women do tend to think differently.

Women gather and integrate details more quickly, consider more options in solving problems, and tend to take a more contextual perspective when considering an issue. Female brains tend to think in webs more than lines (Cool). This means that rather than thinking through a problem in a more predictable logical sequence, you're likely to be reminded of many different associated concepts, some of which may prompt creative new ideas. Orthopedic surgeon Taryn Rose is a good example. She saw an opportunity to use her medical expertise in designing attractive and comfortable shoes for women. Her business, Taryn Rose Shoes, became so successful that she sold it for $40 million in 2008, and she has been featured on Oprah, NPR's All Things Considered, and Good Morning America. If you have the chance to wear her shoes, you would find them stylish, comfortable and good for your feet. All of that came from her creative non-linear thinking—most surgeons don't think of fashion as their business or consider stylish shoe design as a way to improve the public's foot health. Are there some ideas that are rolling around in your head that could be turned into an innovative business?

Every individual is different, but overall, the research is clear—we as women bring certain strengths to leading that help us develop as transformational leaders. In today's world, executives in some workplaces and industries still look askance at leadership approaches they perceive as touchy-feely, weak or just plain feminine. But times are changing. We now have the chance to build on our strengths so that we can create positive transformation at work and in our lives.

As Jessica and I worked together on her career strategy, it became clear that her chances of achieving her dream of becoming the CFO and a transformational leader in her current position were slim. Fortunately, Jessica received an opportunity from a new company where she would report directly to the CFO. He spoke throughout the interview about the organization's values and the importance of creating an engaged and committed culture at the company. The organization also has several diversity initiatives that support women accelerating their careers.

Jessica took the position and is now leading a global finance team that centralizes all financial services and integrates them across the company. Jessica's team has a tremendous impact on key performance metrics and employee engagement scores are high. She learned to use her natural strengths as a leader, rather than the learned behaviors of the traditional dominant style that served her poorly in her last position. She is more aware of her own emotions and the impact she has on others.

 # 5 Strategies to Seize Success While Practicing Transformational Leadership

Here are five approaches to use to develop your abilities as a transformational leader. As you read, see which appeal to you as an approach with which you can experiment.

 ## Action A: Build trust

When you work in a trusting environment, you feel energetic and productive. You know that others give you the benefit of the doubt and support you. They have your back, and you feel it. Trust is the building block of all great teams and relationships. It's impossible to be a transformational leader without being able to build and maintain a base of trust with those you lead.

How can you build trust? Trust develops when you consistently show up as who you say you are and follow through on the commitments you make. You build trust when your behavior aligns with the promises you make. If you make a promise and can't fulfill it, you can recover most times by telling the person you made the promise to that you need to re-negotiate what you can do in the changing situation. For example, say you told your team that you would have all their performance reviews completed by the end of the 4th quarter. A couple of weeks later, you receive a big project and the demands of working on it begin taking a toll on other priorities. Instead of letting the deadline you communicated slide, you would update your team and make sure people know that you need to re-negotiate your prior promise, and why. Great leaders are transparent and communicate directly with others.

Many organizations have stated values that serve as guiding principles. Whether used actively as behavioral guidelines or not. You build trust as a leader when you reinforce and hold yourself and others accountable for acting in alignment with the organization or team's stated values. For example, if one of the values is "integrity" or "doing the right thing," model it consistently and address situations where someone on the team behaved in violation of that value. In turn, reward and recognize them when they display integrity too. As we developed your personal values in the Right Focus chapter, I recommend that you use the organization's values as a framework for how you, your co-workers and your team treat each other. If you don't have clear values in your company, develop your values with your team.

A clear, powerful, and true values statement guides individual behaviors and decisions. It creates boundaries for what are acceptable ways to solve problems and achieve goals. Your values statement makes it clear to people how they should treat each other and how they should treat customers. If you stay consistent with it and talk about the values often, you will build and enhance trust.

A clearly defined statement of values enables your team or organization to:

- Define appropriate behaviors
- Help you know if they are doing the right things
- Guide you to make right decisions
- Attract, recruit and select people who share those values
- Reward those who exemplify the values consistently, and hold accountable those who do not.
- Narrow the gap between actual values and desired values

Here's an example of a value statement for your team or organization:

- Integrity: Be fair, honest and do the right thing.
- Customer focus: Exceed customer expectations.
- Collaboration: Work together and support each other.
- Innovation: Dare to think big and then make it happen.
- Excellence: Never be content with less than your best.

Once you have a clear statement of your values, you and everyone involved can use this information to determine the ways you agree to behave with each other.

Here are some questions that you can ask your team to develop your team values:

1. What are the things you value deeply about working with our team or organization? What do our customers value about working with us?
2. What's the one value that without it, our team/organization would not be the same?
3. What do you think our core values are?

Look for common themes and select the top 3 to 5 core values that best represent your team or organization's guiding principles.

If you already have core values for your team or company, you can drill deeper to develop the value behaviors for each value. Behaviors here are defined as specific, observable or verifiable. For each value, ask three powerful questions:

1. What behaviors do **NOT** reflect the value of ....?
2. What will we be saying and doing with each other that demonstrates our commitment to this value?
3. What will we be saying and doing with our customers (internal and external) that demonstrates our commitment to this value?

By developing the value behaviors, you build a values communications tool that outlines what you are committing to; you can use it to manage performance, onboard new hires, and coach and develop others.

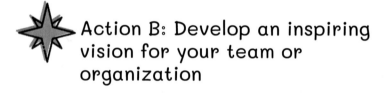 ## Action B: Develop an inspiring vision for your team or organization

Transformational leaders inspire others with a compelling vision for the future. Remember the exercise in the Right Focus chapter, in which you developed your personal vision for yourself and your career? This time, do the same thing, but for your organization or the team with which you work. Vision answers the question "If you were transported three to five years into the future and your highest wishes for this team or organization were realized, what would you see?" What is your long-term picture of success for your area of responsibility? Can you describe it in a way that gets others excited?

Unlike a mission statement, which describes your team or organization's purpose, a vision statement sets a standard or overriding goal that you aspire to; once fulfilled, it's critical to formulate a new vision for which to reach. The first step in developing your vision is to bring together key stakeholders to reflect on the best future state they can see for your team or organization. Use a guided imagery question like:

Imagine yourself waking up in the future three to five years from now. As you walk around your company, notice what people are saying and doing, what they are accomplishing together, what others (customers, your industry, employees, the media, the community) are saying about you and what heights you've reached as a team or organization.

Before discussing observations with your group, have everyone write down their specific description of exactly what they saw as they walked around in the future—no matter how far-fetched. Instruct them to be as detailed as possible and to be unafraid to use vivid descriptions of what they experienced in this time-travel exercise.

Once everyone has a chance to get their ideas down, encourage a dialogue that helps you find a common foundation for building a vision that unites your stakeholders.

- Form groups of eight to ten for large groups, three to five for smaller ones.
- Within each group, ask each person to share his or her vision of the Best Future State. This process promotes a thoughtful dialogue about what each person visualized.
- Ask the groups to summarize the common themes across the vision descriptions they've heard in their group.
- Instruct the groups to report these "vision themes" to the large group. Some of the most frequently mentioned common themes in the sub-groups revolve around things like what the workplace would look like, what customers would be experiencing, the company's growth, collective learning, impact on society, winning awards, and being voted a great place to work.

- If possible, a skilled facilitator can support you by ensuring the groups' input is encouraged, captured, processed and reported back later; this frees you up to participate fully.

Here's an example of common themes generated by a team:

- Caliber of staff
- Recognition of being the undisputed leader
- Growth—best practices
- Customer satisfaction at an all-time high
- Employees are fully engaged
- Outdoing the competition
- Deeper/expanded offering

By starting with each individual's vivid description of the future and moving to the agreed-upon common themes across all the sub-groups, you will be able to identify a compelling vision. The vision statement itself is the overall umbrella that answers the questions, "What are we going after?" and "What is our big goal that will take us to that future state?"

A historical example is when John Kennedy said "We will have a man on the moon;" he added: "And it will be done before the end of this decade." That was an inspiring vision that NASA visualized and bench-marked. We did in fact accomplish this vision in less than 10 years. Some say that when that vision was achieved, our space program floundered because there wasn't another compelling vision developed to take its place.

The common themes give you the details and build ownership. The big goal or vision statement provides direction and is the framework for your strategic plan. Here are the criteria for writing a great vision statement for you to consider:

- Is it future-oriented?
- Does it set a standard of excellence?
- Is it ambitious enough? Too ambitious?

- Can you communicate it often with passion?
- Is it readily understandable?
- Can it inspire enthusiasm and commitment?

Make your vision something you can benchmark and break into milestones over a span of time – eventually leading you to achieve the final big goal.

Action C: Create meaning for others

Would you take less money if you could work at something that you found interesting, engaging or challenging? If you're like most people, you would. A 2018 Harvard Business Review study found that "More than 9 out of 10 employees… are willing to trade a percentage of their lifetime earnings for greater meaning at work. Across age and salary groups, workers want meaningful work badly enough that they're will-ing to pay for it" (Achor et al.).

You can create meaning for others by how you describe, position and reinforce the work to be done. Let's go back to the space pro-gram mentioned in the vision example earlier. There's an old story you can find in multiple sources about a janitor at NASA who was asked by a curious visitor what he did at the organization. (In some versions of the story, the visitor is John F. Kennedy). The janitor responded without hesitation, "We're putting a man on the moon." He was excited and proud of his work because he saw himself as a member of a team doing incredible things. The janitor saw the relationship between what he did, keeping the place clean, and this mission-critical project.

Use your vision and its description to show others how what they are doing is important and contributes to the broader whole. Sometimes we get so wrapped up in the day-to-day accomplishment of tasks, we forget that we are contributing to something bigger. You can lose motivation when work starts feeling like a meaningless series of "to do's." You as a transformational leader can make all the difference by reminding others why what they are doing is important and how it fits into the bigger vision.

You also create meaning by celebrating successes along the way. When milestones are reached, are you acknowledging people on the team for their accomplishments? Are you making people who put their all into advancing the vision—even in a small way—heroes in the examples you share about the progress you and your team are making? I asked a skilled leader I've worked with about why she seemed so effective in going after big goals and engaging her team. She thought for a minute and said, "I repeat myself a lot. I talk about the vision, why it's important and how recent actions taken by my team support it. I thank people for the specific things they do and give examples. Then I get up the next day and do the same thing again." Creating meaning isn't a one-time event. It's a habit that, if you develop it, reaps benefits for all.

 ## Action D: Lead change

Transformational leaders look for the opportunity in change. They ask: "What changes do we want or need to make?" and "How will we benefit from making those changes?" When you adopt a transformational style of leadership, you don't waste energy resisting change, but focus on using it to collectively create something new.

Often when people initiate change, they give an analysis of some sort in an attempt to influence *thinking*. That's not enough. It's not that the data isn't important, but accessing *feeling* is essential to effective behavioral change. The first step in leading change is to create a sense of urgency. You can do this by identifying what the potential crisis is or what the opportunity might be.

Developing a sense of urgency gets employees out of their comfort zone. One organization I worked with had a problem with not listening to their customers. One of the managers videotaped an angry customer and played it for other managers as well as the employees. Seeing the incident on tape created a collective sense of "we have to do something." The response was visceral, not analytical. What are some of the things you might do to stir emotion around a needed change?

You agree that change is necessary. Now it's time to form a team to guide the change. Who are your strongest people? Do you have them in the right positions? What is your common goal or picture of change success? Once you address these questions, it's time for you and your team to develop a plan to get there and execute.

A leader's role in change management is to empower action by removing roadblocks and helping the team create short term wins. You need to consider factors such as: What projects or initiatives should be selected first? Which have the highest chance of initial success? What resources are available? A leader takes time to reinforce, recognize and celebrate progress. You create momentum towards your ultimate goal when employees are engaged and feel supported.

As a leader, you are also seen as a model for others, so it's critical that you model resilience. That means admitting mistakes, changing your plans in response to changing circumstances, and sticking to your vision despite the challenges that arise in the short term. Look for opportunities to let your team see you doing those things.

The following are actions you can take to effectively lead change:

1. Create a sense of urgency
2. Find the right team and put people in the right positions
3. Engage your team, define your picture of success and set a common goal
4. Develop a plan (short- and long-term)

5. Remove obstacles

6. Celebrate short-term wins

7. Demonstrate resilience

 # Action E: Be an effective coach

The best leaders make coaching and developing others a priority. When you were asked to think back on a coach or a past boss who positively impacted you, you likely recalled fond memories of how you felt in the presence of that person and ways that you grew.

There are three main purposes of coaching:

- Reinforce performance
- Improve performance
- Model or teach performance

In coaching others around performance, it's critical for each of your team members to have a clear picture of your expectations of both their individual goals and the team goals. It's your job as leader to monitor and track performance, recognizing successes as well as addressing mistakes and shortcomings.

One tool we introduced to clients to help them give both positive and developmental performance feedback is a process we call EAR. EAR stands for outlining Expectations, acknowledging the Action that the person took or did not take, and defining the end Result. For example, suppose you have an employee named Carol. One of Carol's goals is to develop an onboarding process for new employees by the end of the quarter. You asked Carol for progress reports and haven't received any. As far as you know, Carol doesn't appear to have started working on her goal, and it's half-way through the quarter. You overhear Carol tell a colleague that she is swamped with other work and hasn't started. In using the EAR format, you could say:

"Carol, I'm anxious to see the work you've accomplished on your goal of developing a new onboarding process. We agreed that you would be updating me on your progress. We are halfway through the quarter and I haven't received an update. I'm concerned that you may not be as far along with this project as I had hoped. If we don't launch an improved process next quarter, the hires we'll be making won't receive the attention and information they deserve. Can I help you in some way?"

EAR Worksheet Process

Instructions: Prepare an EAR Worksheet for an employee whose performance you wish to recognize or to improve. Remember to record the following:

Expectation or situation: This may be a restatement of a performance expectation or a description of the specific situation you encountered or observed.

Action: These are the specific actions you or another employee/associate took in the situation. These statements record behaviors, not assumptions.

Results: These are the outcomes or results of your or another employee/associate's actions.

 Seizing Success: Sue's Story

Sue is a transformational leader. She heads the compliance department for a school that educates students in preparation for healthcare careers and participates in one of our Key Women's Leadership Forums. Other parts of the organization do not always embrace Sue as the Chief Compliance Officer. Sue's department performs internal audits, administers tests to make sure the school is doing the right things in a variety of areas and examines student outcomes. "The role of compliance can be viewed as that of a rule enforcer," Sue explained. "How do you deliver less-than good news like 'You're not teaching as directly to the stated outcomes as you need to be?'"

Upon starting in her role, Sue had a simple and inspirational vision: Quality is #1, and we are the keepers of quality. Her team often discussed and posted reminders throughout the department such as: "What's tolerated today becomes acceptable tomorrow" and "You accept what you condone." Compliance had a clear end goal—quality first. Sue added, "that translates into student satisfaction." Sue created meaning for her staff by showing why what they do is important to the organization and its "customers" (students).

Sue doesn't stop there. She coaches team members on how to present feedback, minimize defensiveness and develop a positive mindset. She sees her team's role as reducing risk by identifying areas of opportunity and offering help. Her approach transformed the way other parts of the organization view compliance, and inspired her team to perform at the highest levels.

Sue challenges herself in her personal life, too. I didn't think I was hearing her correctly when she told me she runs in 100-mile races—"What did you say?" I blurted out. "How long did it take you?" I pursued. "Twenty-eight hours," she replied.

Sue is an over-50, vibrant woman with incredible resilience. She has non-Hodgkin's lymphoma and survived a skydiving accident where she suffered several broken bones and multiple surgeries. Always pushing herself to be her personal best, Sue recently trained for her next big race, a 150-mile run. That might sound like a nightmare to most, but in her words, "it's been a dream of mine." Sue's approach to achieving her personal big goal was similar as to how she worked to transform the compliance area at work—holding a positive picture or vision, building trust, adapting to change and developing herself and others.

The race was actually 152.25 miles. As Sue trained for it, our women's forum got regular updates from Sue on her training and progress.

She got up at 3:30am and ran most mornings to prepare. She put in a full day at work, ate nourishing meals to replenish herself, and worked diligently with a world-class coach to maintain her strength and stamina.

Sue ran her big race in 39 hours, 43 minutes and 51 seconds, having stayed up a total of 46 hours without sleep. She came in first and was the only woman in the race! Sue now holds the all-time female record for this 150-mile race and has the second-fastest time as well.

When I spoke with Sue to congratulate her on this amazing feat, I asked her to share some of the keys to her success in the 150-mile race. I think each applies to our lives professionally and personally.

Here are some of Sue's insights:

- "I visualized each 25-mile segment ahead of the race, seeing myself feeling good and completing it," Sue shared. "I set up my mind for success ahead of time." She visualized what she would feel like and her progress at each segment as she practiced for the race. Sue commented that during the race she felt a familiarity with reaching her short-term goal for each loop in the race even though she had only practiced the actual run in her mind.

- Self-awareness is key to athletic performance at the competitive level. Why? Because each athlete has specific psychological stumbling blocks that can hold them back—fears or negative self-talk that can cause them to hold back when they need to be pushing themselves their hardest and blocking out distractions. Recognizing these factors and finding effective ways to handle them is key to turning in the best performance you're capable of. "I continuously reminded myself that I'm stronger than my fears," Sue said.

When I asked what her biggest fear was, she easily answered, "not finishing—I didn't want the regret of not completing the race." In Sue's daunting run there were alligators and coyotes roaming her path, as well as the wall of psychological fatigue that can play tricks on your mind. "I kept remembering the 'why' behind what I was doing and used the mantra of 'head down, stay focused, stay focused,' – that made all the difference," Sue shared. She alternatively used a second affirmation, "through grit and grace, I'll get this done."

- We know that team sports like baseball and basketball thrive on camaraderie, but what about solo events? It turns out that the same principle is true. Sue had a team of four support people who were stationed on the run. They were inspired by Sue's passion to complete the 150-mile race. Being inspired to provide for Sue wasn't enough. She set specific parameters for them, as she does with her compliance team at work, which helped Sue beat the past female record. "When I stop, I can't be there for more than 5 minutes and I expect that you will be prepared with my food," Sue had instructed her team. "If they aren't prepared, I told the team that I'd run past them; it was their job to run and catch up to me so that I could eat." Sue had clear expectations for her team and bonded with them in a way that made them feel like part of an incredible athletic achievement even though they themselves weren't running. It paid off. She feels that her 5-minute pit stops helped her to beat the past female record by 9 minutes and 38 seconds.

Being a woman didn't hold Sue back in a sport that's heavily male-dominated—it may have even helped. Ultimately, both Sue and Jessica were able to achieve their big large-scale goals, not by being perfect or emulating the most successful men in their fields, but by tapping in to traits like self-awareness, trust-building, communication and collaboration.

Review the five growth strategies in this chapter

You can enhance your leadership capabilities by developing a transformational leadership style. Here are the strategies we covered in this chapter:

A. Build trust

B. Develop an inspiring vision for your team or organization

C. Create meaning for others

D. Lead change

E. Be an effective coach

Take Action: Experiment and consider these questions

Leadership is about going first and supporting those who count on you. Here are some questions that you might ask yourself as you think about how you want to lead now and in the future:

1. What is my leadership philosophy?
2. What are my strengths as a leader, and how can I build on them?
3. How could I communicate my vision for my team in an inspiring way?
4. Do I lead change or resist it? What are some examples?
5. How can I model the behaviors I expect from others?

Transformational leadership takes commitment. It's not a short-term fix, but a way of leading. Like any healthy habit, if you practice it over time, it becomes a part of you. One of the ways you can reinforce the development of a transformational leadership style is to have the support of like-minded peers. In the next chapter, you will learn more about creating your own personal support team.

Alone, we can do so little.
Together we can do so much.

-

Helen Keller

Chapter 7:

Power of Peers — Your Support Team

I recall a time when a CEO in one of the peer forums I facilitated presented a business issue and projected flat growth over the upcoming year. She was about to go on to what she thought was her bigger issue when one of her peers said, "Wait a minute—why are you assuming that your company won't grow? Your intention dictates what happens. So, if you plan to have a flat year, just give up and go play tennis."

I've seen some hard-driving CEOs come to their peer group with an issue that initially appears cut-and-dried. When they examine it with the group and listen to the feedback, it confronts them with new alternatives that weren't evident before. Part of the feedback the CEO who projected flat growth heard from her peer group included challenges such as "Be honest with yourself and don't play the victim" and "Is this a self-fulfilling prophecy?" The feedback opened the door for the CEO to remove her blinders and see alternatives for growing the business. Indeed, she grew her business 12% that year, something she couldn't have done without the outside view and push from her peer forum.

We get stuck in our own thinking. Even people who are incredibly talented and skilled in every other aspect of their profession are missing out on a key skill—soliciting and listening to ideas from trusted peers.

 ## What we know

One of the hallmarks of effective leadership is the ability to distance yourself from a work or personal situation and to look at it with non-attachment. By "helicoptering" over an issue, problem, or decision, you are more objective because you see the situation from a less self-centered view. When you look at what's going on from a distance and minimize the "it's about me" factor, you improve your critical thinking and decision-making and often find new and creative alternatives.

So how do you develop the ability to stay detached from a situation, allowing yourself to look at the key factors from a new perspective?

Bringing your situation, problem, decision, or idea to a peer group made up of people you trust is among the most effective methods I've observed. I've seen some participants achieve their personal and professional goals while others struggled with internal flaws that led to their companies stagnating, or worse. I learned what separates the successful ones from their less successful counterparts, and with Dennis Stearns, wrote a book called *CEO Road Rules: Right Focus, Right People, Right Execution* to share our findings. One key finding indicated that synergy occurs when leaders from diverse backgrounds come together for the purpose of becoming "even better" leaders at their companies. Some call this type of collaboration a CEO or key leader roundtable or advisory board experience. Others call it a "mastermind" group. Coined by Napoleon Hill in his book *Think and Grow Rich*, a mastermind group is a peer-to-peer mentoring exchange where members help each other solve problems and achieve goals with one another's input, advice and support.

What does becoming "even better" mean to you? The focus of an effective forum is to help you and your organization move from where you are to where you want to be. Being part of a forum involves growing personally and professionally. "Even better" is about helping you to evolve into your personal best and take your organization to new heights. It's about learning exponentially from trusted advisors. Exponential learning involves an investment of your energy up front, even to make minimal progress. Over time and with effort, your progress accelerates and might continue to do so without substantial additional effort, like the "fly wheel" effect outlined in *Good to Great* by Jim Collins.

We could use new framing

You may be thinking, "And when do I find time I already don't have to meet with a peer support group?" When even day-to-day tasks are exhausting, taking even more time to think about your large-scale goals and leadership style may seem impossible. Often, women have a conditioned response to a sense of overwhelming challenge by putting it on the back burner and dealing with it "later"—which may never come.

Actually, taking time to connect with your vision and mission is all the more important for women. Studies show that organizations with more senior-ranking women have a competitive edge. Women at such companies have the ability to collaborate and seek advice from each other, enhancing their leadership skills. Most organizations are still male-dominated at the top, however, meaning that type of collaboration doesn't always happen organically.

Recent research also demonstrates that women in business who seek out peer support groups are happier and more successful than those who do not (Shapiro and Bottary) (Uzzi). Being among supportive peers who understand your pressures and challenges reduces your stress. As one of our members in the Key Women's Leadership Forum put it, "It's like being with your best girlfriends, but they understand what you do!"

What's the power of these groups? Women CEOs and C-Suite executives have some unique challenges. Here are some of the frustrations that women we work with in leadership roles have expressed:

- "You begin to question your own abilities when the men at work don't support you."
- "I'm not sure people would see me as a leader if they knew the real me."
- "Do I really deserve this?"
- "How can I balance everything with work and family?"
- "I don't seem to get the same level of respect that men in my role do."
- "I feel like I have to prove myself every time. A man can walk in and it's assumed that he's qualified by virtue of just holding the position."

Women, and human beings in general, feel less upset about challenges and perceived obstacles when they know others share those concerns and experiences. One of the underlying principles of group therapy is that the participants realize others struggle with the same issues and challenges. Their experiences are more common than they thought. The universality of experiences somehow makes them more acceptable instead of being ignored or hidden. Talking with supportive peers helps women in leadership realize that they are not alone and don't have to be perfect to succeed at work or in life. This makes all the difference.

Better options for peer support in your life

In facilitating CEO roundtables, I watch members develop a professional intimacy and deep trust in one another. I see leaders do courageous things because of the support and smart observations shared by their roundtable members. In order to achieve these results, you need a certain kind of group. There are three key ingredients to a successful and meaningful executive forum experience:

- **Right Focus:** The group is purposeful—they learn to work "on" their businesses or careers, not just "in" them
- **Right People:** The group comprises a diverse mix of leaders who want to be their personal and professional best and are willing to share their insights with others
- **Right Execution:** The group serves as an accountability system that ensures implementation, and a seasoned facilitator supports the group in deeper exploration of relevant issues and future directions

By creating a focused process to address problems and opportunities, the group can go deeper faster. Using the power of peers to its greatest advantage, you create a confidential environment where trust can build. Group members often start out as strangers who aren't part of the same industry or social circle—and that's actually a plus. Whether a peer group is made up of CEOs, executive women, or people in other leadership positions, it is a platform for distancing yourself from those who may want to direct the outcome, such as your spouse, business partner, other employees or board members. It also affords the opportunity to see things in a new light.

People who aren't your boss, co-workers or family don't come at a problem with the same assumptions. Your peers have no vested interest in advising you a certain way; they share their experience more objectively. For instance, Maria, one of the entrepreneurial women in our all-female forum, brought an issue to the group about expansion of her company. Her CFO recommended closing down one of their product lines to reduce risk while expanding. By contrast, her Chief Marketing Officer felt that the new branding would dramatically increase sales of the product line over time and help cash flow. Maria respected her team members' views, but after hearing the depth and breadth of feedback from an independent group of executive women, she realized that the

CFO and CMO's perspectives were too inwardly focused. Each reflected only the officer's respective functional area. She needed a wider view, and that's what she got from the forum. After receiving some great feedback on developing a growth strategy, Maria ultimately decided to take a different path where she combined several product lines and focused the branding efforts on one of the lucrative product lines resulting in new profits and expanded services.

Diverse perspectives are important, but to get the most benefit from discussions you need a peer group whose members have some things in common. I used to believe that convening a separate women's leadership peer group was not necessary, and that mixed groups of CEOs or key leaders were adequate. I changed my thinking. When I started leading all-female groups I saw that something special happened—women brought up problems and feelings they were reluctant to share in mixed-gender groups. For instance, Patricia added background about an issue she brought up in her forum regarding a high-stakes presentation and how to improve next time. She shared that on the morning of the big day she felt hurried because she had to get her children ready for a school play, got stuck in traffic, and literally ran to the meeting room to start in the nick of time. Patricia felt the empathy in the room from her peers and commented that she wouldn't have felt comfortable giving such details to other groups. She received some great feedback not only on improving her presentation, but on strategies for improved work-life integration.

Using a more integrated approach with the focus on the whole person differs from the more traditional peer forum model because work and life aren't segregated. Women want to address all areas of their lives, not just work. I found my mostly male CEO groups much more focused on running their businesses, getting scalable, obtaining funding, and developing an exit strategy—all important, but a definite business focus. When we started the Key Women's Leadership Forum, we wanted to bring women in leadership roles together to focus on the whole self: career, mind, body, and spirit.

One Big Strategy to Seize Success

 ## Action: Form a Forum

Peer forums for executive-level leaders offer an antidote for the truism that "It's lonely at the top." There are no work peers for CEOs within their organizations. That same dynamic plays out all the more for many women in leadership roles. They're usually in the minority, and often the only woman on an executive team. Women in leadership are frequently called upon to coach and mentor other women in their organizations. They usually don't have a vehicle for getting individualized support and development geared specifically for them. Women feel pressure to perform (as discussed in the previous chapter), and often lack a support system to get feedback on challenges or opportunities they face.

There's more to assembling the perfect group other than gender. Since tapping into the members' collective intelligence and experience is your goal, the best peer groups are made up of people who consistently raise the bar for themselves and others. They are learners who want to grow and influence the growth of others. They also hold themselves and others accountable. The group process becomes an accountability system to enhance execution of agreed-upon next steps.

For example, after a participant in one of our peer forums brings an issue or opportunity to the group, I always ask them, "What are the 2 to 3 things you heard in the feedback that you plan to act on?" They state them, I capture the actions they've committed to, and at the next meeting ask them to update the members on their progress. The group remembers and often compliments progress or remarks on lack of effort; either way, the person with the issue is motivated to continue acting on what they say is important. For instance, the CEO who initially projected no growth for the year was challenged by the group. She changed her thinking about accepting that the market for her business would be down in the upcoming year and brainstormed alternatives with her executive team. They created a plan to buck the trend in the industry and stepped up their ecommerce initiatives to increase sales, bringing the CEO's actions into closer alignment with her ambitions and her ultimate vision for the company. With the group's help, she remained on track with that plan.

Why haven't peer support groups become part of best practices for supporting women in leadership? There's evidence they're starting to catch on. Sheryl Sandburg's book *Lean In* promotes the idea, and her Lean In Foundation, started in 2013, boasts that there are now 37,000 "Lean In Circles" around the country. The website Meetup.com allows users to find all-female peer support groups with a variety of focuses from Seattle to Singapore.

There may be one near you already. What if you can't find one or it isn't the right fit for you? Consider starting your own group—either one that meets in person or, if there aren't enough potential members who can realistically meet in person, a virtual group. Either way, identify professional women whom you want to have in your peer group. Consider bright women you met at conferences or in other business situations. A group size of 6 to 8 works best for a virtual meeting to create intimacy and also give more airtime in a shorter meeting structure.

You can structure your group's meetings by starting with updates where each participant takes 3 minutes to update the group on their biggest opportunities and challenges professionally and personally. Next you might adapt the format used by the Key Women's Leadership Forum (see Appendix A on page 171) on how to bring issues or opportunities to your group. Schedule in-person meetings for 2.5 to 3 hours once a month so you have a regular rhythm as you meet. Because it's harder to stay engaged for longer than 1.5 hours virtually, schedule virtual meetings for 60 to 90 minutes and consider holding them twice a month. Google Hangout, Zoom, or Go to Webinar can assist you in setting up the right technology.

Here's a more detailed example of how the women's forum addresses issues and some of the outcomes.

 ## Seizing Success: Amy's Story

Amy was a 20-year veteran at a publicly traded, entrepreneurially minded entertainment company, and only one of two female executives. She and her marketing team had passion for their work and highly specialized skills in the niche that they served. When the market for their services suffered a downturn, the organization started to lose revenue and the board opted to sell to a foreign-owned company in an adjacent market. They revamped the leadership team, the culture changed, and Amy was asked to downsize the team that she valued so highly.

The changes made for a grueling work environment with miscommunication from executives and layoffs a regular occurrence. In the midst of the chaos, one of Amy's male peers began using the uncertainty to his political advantage by attempting to discredit her. He made false claims about her when she wasn't present and used non-verbals like eye-rolls when people would bring up her name. Amy's job was intact, but her confidence had been shaken and her team was in disarray with their morale at an all-time low.

Amy was frustrated at work and did not have the work/life alignment she needed to feel purposeful and satisfied. As she looked to the future of her career, she considered her options. She could weather the storm at the company that she had been loyal to for over a decade, or leave to pursue something new and make a fresh start.

When Amy initially presented her issue to her forum, the group asked many questions. Here's a sampling:

"What has kept you committed to this company so long?"

"What excites you most about your profession? Your current position?"

"Why do you think your colleague is discrediting you?"

Next, each forum member shared their observations and feedback. In discussion, they immediately jumped in to offer their support and share their wisdom to help Amy design her strategy. Her group consisted of women from various industries and different roles—among them a chief operating officer, a sales executive, a human resources VP, an entrepreneur, a CFO, general counsel, and a partner in an accounting firm. All of the women in the group had a wealth of business knowledge and a strict commitment to the confidentiality code of ethics agreed to by all the forum participants.

The group used Key Associates' (KA) Career Criteria Decision Guide to structure their feedback for Amy. They asked her to think about the numerous facets of her job satisfaction and to outline the criteria she would use to weigh decisions affecting her future career. Among the criteria that Amy set were:

- **Learning and Growth**: taking the opportunity to go beyond her current skill set and expertise.
- **Purposeful Work**: engaging in meaningful action that plays to her strengths and passion.
- **Work/Life Alignment**: bringing her work, home life, and personal desires into harmony.
- **Achievement**: challenging herself and others to attain a new standard of excellence.
- **Developing Others**: finding the opportunity to coach and mentor others.
- **Financial Stability**: making enough to support her family and save toward her kids' college and her own retirement.

The process guided the group to look at Amy's issue at a deep level and to use decision criteria that are unique to female executives who balance the rigorous demands of work and home.

Applying the information they uncovered, Amy's Key Women's Leadership Forum used the deep exploration of Amy's situation to encourage her to remain in her role as SVP of Marketing. They discovered that despite the temporary challenges she faced, her current position fit the majority of her criteria for career satisfaction. There was a lot to be salvaged, and the group worked together to help her design a different approach to her situation. To weather the storm, Amy designed a plan for her own success that included:

- Scheduling time with each team member to understand their concerns and fears and listen to their ideas about the future.
- Being more assertive with her undermining colleague when he attempted political moves.
- Setting boundaries and expectations with the various players on the leadership team to foster more effective communication.
- Designing succinct messaging to communicate corporate changes to her marketing team and rebuild morale.
- Changing her outlook to emphasize the long-term positive aspects of her work rather than focusing on the immediate challenges of the acquisition.

These positive changes and refreshed approach got Amy through several tough quarters at her company. Her willingness to adjust and to drive her team in challenging circumstances was ultimately rewarded. Amy received a promotion to head a new division of the company.

 ## Review the BIG growth strategy in this chapter

 Identify women who are your peers and see if they are interested in a Mastermind or Peer Forum.

 At your first meeting, set communication guidelines with each other and sign a confidentiality statement (examples in Appendices B & C).

Meet regularly—once a month for three hours is a good rhythm.

 Use an agreed-upon process of bringing issues or opportunities to the group.

 Consider hiring a professional facilitator or coach to convene your meetings.

Take Action: Experiment and consider these questions

Just as Amy received feedback that helped to improve and enhance her career, you can learn more about yourself and your next steps by accessing the power of peers. Here are some questions to explore with a trusted colleague or group of female peers:

1. Are there some past dreams or career fantasies that I've left behind? How do they appeal to me now?
2. Am I aligning these in a meaningful way in my current position or career? Why or why not?
3. What are some ways I can use the group's support?
4. What are some current issues or opportunities that I'd like help sorting out?
5. What are some career/life possibilities that I haven't thought about?

People often get so wrapped up in the work at hand and making it through the demands of the day that they put on hold the opportunity to explore what's purposeful for them. I encourage you to consider these questions. Even if you don't involve anyone else, this action experiment is something you can journal about to discover next steps for you.

Conclusion:

As women, the climate is right for us to take the lead in our own lives, in the workplace, and on the world stage. My intention has been to engage you in a broader conversation and encourage you to reflect on what it takes for you to succeed as a leader as well as offer expertise, resources and action strategies that will make a difference in your career and life. Hopefully after reading about the struggles and successes of the women featured in this book, you are inspired to assess where you are now in relation to where you want to be in your life and use the book's guidance to help you get there.

The first three chapters of the book focused on the important intra-personal foundation for leadership – having confidence, finding your personal and professional focus and handling the pressure to perform that we face as women in particular. The middle chapters were designed to help you enhance your interactions with others as a leader through improving your assertiveness and developing your ability to influence others more consistently. The last two chapters outline how you can build on the strengths women excel in to become a transformational leader and find the peer support you need to stay strong and grow in a challenging environment.

Transformational leadership by its definition builds on strengths that women inherently bring to the workplace. The time is right for us as women to come forward and use our considerable talents to seize success, not only for ourselves but for those we lead. Are you ready to move forward and take the risk?

Your feedback is so important to me. I would appreciate hearing back from you and learning about how you've applied some of the strategies in this book. In turn, I'd enjoy hearing about your insights and favorite strategies to grow as a leader.

Please visit: www.SeizeSuccesses.com

In addition, there's an assessment you can take on the website that will help you assess which of the competency areas you are strongest in and which you might want to target to develop.

You or your organization may want some coaching support or help in setting up a women's forum. I'm also a frequent speaker on leadership and available to talk about women and leadership to your organization or company.

For more information, please contact me directly at:
mary@keyassociatesinc.com

Acknowledgements

Our early years shape who we become. I want to acknowledge and thank my mother Helen Warakomski, my grandmothers, Eva Warakomski and Bernice Witkowski, and my sister Joan Land for the love, nurturing and support they provided. I learned a lot about what it is to become a woman and how to live independently from being with these wonderful women.

My early education was shaped by some smart and dedicated nuns from the Franciscan Order – Sister Viola, Sister Fidencia and others. They taught me how to reflect and be disciplined in completing projects. Later in my career two mentors/coaches stand out as having the biggest impact on me as a person and as a professional. I'm grateful to Drs. Bernie Berenson and Nido Qubein for the opportunity to learn from them and their guidance at critical periods in my life.

Thank you, Lewis Key, my dear loving husband, who helps me in so many ways. Your keen eye for editing along with your generous nature supported me throughout this process as I became absorbed with writing this book. I want to acknowledge our furry cat family for the comfort and gentle support their presence provides – Santini, Sophia and Princess, I love you.

I'd like to tell my loyal and loving friends how much the time they devoted to hearing about this book and their insightful feedback has meant to me – Cathy Taylor, Carol Maier, Randy Baskerville, Michael Donovan, Alan Briskin, Sharon Jordan-Evans, Cecelia Houser, Jesse Stoner, Stewart Levine and Carol Briggs.

Writing a book is never a solitary activity. Thank you to Emily Hines for her fantastic editing, Nancy Breuer for her help in setting up a structure, Karen Rowe for helping me to self-publish, Diana Flores for her engaging graphics and design and my amazing office manager, Wendy Herlache, who handles our business with competent caring and supports me in all I do.

I want to express my gratitude to the fabulous women who participate in our Key Women's Leadership Forum. You have inspired this book and I treasure the intimacy we share and the opportunity to watch each other grow. A big thank you to our forum team of facilitators for their talent, caring and outstanding facilitation and coaching – Laura Scott, Dr. Jen Hall and new to our team, Gerri Vereen – I couldn't do this without you.

Appendices

Appendix A: Forum Issue

Key Associates, Inc.
Helping Leaders and Organizations Grow

NAME: _____ DATE: _____

1. Summarize the issue you'll discuss with the forum group (use no more than two sentences). What is the result of successfully addressing the issue?

_____

_____

_____

_____

_____

2. What are the pertinent facts (key points) about your issue that the group needs to know in order to provide the most helpful and relevant feedback?

_____

_____

_____

_____

_____

3. What options, if any, have you considered?

_____

_____

_____

_____

_____

4. What do you want to learn from the group?

_____

_____

_____

_____

_____

5. What will your next steps be?

_____

_____

_____

_____

_____

Appendix B: Guidelines

Key Associates, Inc.
Helping Leaders and Organizations Grow

Engagement Guidelines:

1. Everyone is talking on-point.

2. Build on the comments of other group members.

3. Share openly, honestly and personally.

4. Members are actively listening to each other; let others finish their thought.

5. People disagree respectfully.

6. No one is dominating the discussion.

7. Confidentiality is honored.

8. Phones in purses.

Appendix C: Member Contract

Key Associates, Inc.

Helping Leaders and Organizations Grow

Key Women's Leadership Forum Member Contract

Confidentiality

I commit to maintaining strict confidentiality about what is said in all group sessions and in any discussions with group members away from the group sessions. This includes sharing any information or observations with nonmembers, whether colleagues, partners, spouses, or friends.

Openness

I commit to being open in sharing highly personal matters with members of the group, with the understanding that everything will be held in strictest confidence. If others are not sharing openly with the group, it is my responsibility to raise this with them for discussion within the group. I agree not to push individuals beyond their comfort zone on personally sensitive matters.

Trust

I will join this group with the assumption that its members are worthy of trust. I understand that trust is built through honest, open communications and caring for other members of the group.

Listening

I commit to practicing active listening and to avoid interrupting the member speaking.

Judging Others

I commit to withholding judgment of group members and will avoid giving them unsolicited advice. I will not try to impose my values and beliefs on other members.

Feedback

As a group member, I will offer and receive constructive feedback from others in the group on ideas, behavior, leadership traits and communication styles.

Attendance

I will make every effort to attend all meetings and retreats scheduled for the group, to be on time and to not leave early unless there are extenuating circumstances. Either party may terminate participation in the Key Women's Leadership Forum with 30 days written notice.

Member's signature: _____

Date: _____

References

Chapter 1 References: Confidence

Campbell, Jenna. "Risk: Males vs. Females." *Science in Our World: Certainty and Controversy* (blog). October 23, 2015. **https://sites. psu.edu/siowfa15/2015/10/23/risk-males-vs-females/**

Charness, Gary and Gneezy, Uri, 2012. "Strong Evidence for Gender Differences in Risk Taking." *Journal of Economic Behavior & Organization*, 83(1), 50-58. **http://citeseerx.ist.psu.edu/viewdoc/ download?doi=10.1.1.636.3202&rep=rep1&type=pdf**

Cuddy, Amy. *Presence: Bringing Your Boldest Self to Your Biggest Challenges*. New York: Back Bay Books, 2015.

Dudau, Diana Paula. (2014). The relation between perfectionism and imposter phenomenon. *Procedia: Social and Behavioral Sciences, 127*, 129-133. **https://core.ac.uk/download/pdf/82347725.pdf**

Dweck, Carol. *Mindset: The New Psychology of Success*. New York: Ballantine Books, 2016.

Dyer, Wayne. *The Power of Intention: Learning to Co-Create Your World Your Way.* New York: Hay House, 2004.

George, Bill. *True North: Discover Your Authentic Leadership.* San Francisco: John Wiley & Sons, 2007.

Hawkins, David. *Letting Go: The Pathway of Surrender.* New York: Hay House, 2014.

Kay, Katty, and Claire Shipman. *The Confidence Code: The Art and Science of Self-Assurance.* New York: Harper Business, 2014.

Lillie, Ben. "What we tell ourselves with our body language: Amy Cuddy at TEDGlobal 2012." TedBlog. June 28, 2012. **https://blog.ted.com/what-we-tell-ourselves-with-our-body-language-amy-cuddy-at-tedglobal-2012**

Mather, Mara, and Nicole Lightall. Risk and Reward Are Processed Differently in Decisions Made Under Stress. *Current Directions in Psychological Science*, 2012; 21 (1): 36 DOI: 10.1177/0963721411429452

Nash, Laura, and Howard Stevenson. *Just Enough: Tools for Creating Success in Your Work and Life.* Hoboken, NJ: John Wiley and Sons, 2004.

Vergauwe, Jasmine, Bart Wille, Marjoline Feys, Filip De Fruyt, and Frederik Anseel. "Fear of Being Exposed: The Trait-relatedness of the Imposter Phenomenon and its Relevance in the Work Context." *Journal of Business Psychology*, 2014. DOI: 10.1007/s 10869-014-9382-5.

Wlassoff, Viatcheslav. "Body Language and the Brain: How We Read the Unspoken Signs." BrainBlogger. January 17, 2018. **http://brainblogger.com/2018/01/17/body-language-and-brain-how-we-read-the-unspoken-signs/**

Chapter 2 References: Right Focus

Bennis, Warren. *On Becoming a Leader.* New York: Basic Books, 2009.

George, Bill. *True North: Discover Your Authentic Leadership.* San Francisco: John Wiley & Sons, 2007.

Key, Mary, and Dennis Stearns. *CEO Road Rules: Right Focus, Right People, Right Execution.* Mountain View, CA: Davis-Black Publishing, 2006.

Lieder, Richard. *The Power of Purpose: Find Meaning, Live Longer, Better.* Oakland, CA: Berrett-Koehler, 2010.

McCarthy, Kevin. *On-Purpose Person: Making Your Life Make Sense.* Winter Park, FL: On-Purpose Publishing, 2009.

Pendell, Ryan. "Employee Experience vs. Engagement: What's the Difference?" Gallup Workplace. October 12, 2018. https://www.gallup.com/workplace/243578/employee-experience-engagement-difference.aspx

Chapter 3 References: Pressure to Perform

Alred, Dave. *The Pressure Principle: Handle Stress, Harness Energy and Perform When It Counts.* London: Penguin, 2016.

Ball, Sheryl B., Catherine C. Eckel, Maria Heracleous. "Risk Preferences and Physical Prowess: Is the Weaker Sex More Risk Averse, or Do We Just Think So?" *Journal of Risk and Uncertainty* 41(3): 167-193.

Duncan, Katherine and Daphna Shohamy (2016). "Memory states influence value-based decisions." *Journal of Experimental Psychology* 145 (11): 1420. https://shohamylab.zuckermaninstitute.columbia.edu/sites/default/files/2017-02/Duncan_2016.pdf

Herrick, Lexi. "The True Damage of Second-Shift Motherhood." *Huffpost* (blog). October 1, 2015. https://www.huffingtonpost.com/lexi-herrick/the-true-damage-of-second_b_8224148.html

Kay, Katty, and Claire Shipman. *The Confidence Code: The Art and Science of Self-Assurance.* New York: Harper Business, 2014.

Mather, Mara, and Nicole Lightall. Risk and Reward Are Processed Differently in Decisions Made Under Stress. *Current*

Directions in Psychological Science, 2012; 21 (1): 36
DOI: 10.1177/0963721411429452

Oettingen, Gabriele. *Rethinking Positive Thinking: Inside the New Science of Motivation*. New York: Penguin, 2014.

Rome, David. "Focusing: A Practice to Complement Meditation." *Tricycle*. Fall 2017. **https://tricycle.org/magazine/focusing-2/**

Weisinger, Henrie, and J.P. Pawliw-Fry. *Performing Under Pressure: The Science of Doing Your Best When It Matters Most*. New York: Crown Business, 2015.

Chapter 4 References: Assertiveness

Cuddy, Amy. *Presence: Bringing Your Boldest Self to Your Biggest Challenges*. New York: Back Bay Books, 2015.

Eagly, Alice, and Steven Karau. Role congruity theory of prejudice toward female leaders. *Psychological Review 109*, 573-598. **https://www.rci.rutgers.edu/~search1/pdf/Eagley_Role_Conguity_Theory.pdf**

The Inquiry. "What's the Real Difference Between Men and Women?" Aired May 7, 2018 on BBC World Service. **https://www.bbc.co.uk/programmes/w3cswqt5**

Manning, Margie. "How Women-focused Investments Have Yielded Millions in Returns for the Wwner of Innisbrook." Tampa Bay Business Journal. March 10, 2017. **https://www.bizjournals.com/tampabay/news/2017/03/10/how-women-focused-investments-have-yielded.html**

Sandberg, Sheryl. *Lean In: Women, Work and the Will to Lead*. New York: Alfred A. Knopf, 2013.

"These Are the Women CEOs Leading Fortune 500 Companies." *Fortune*. June 7, 2017. **http://fortune.com/2017/06/07/fortune-500-women-ceos/**

Warner, Judith, and Danielle Corley. "The Women's Leadership Gap." *Center for American Progress.* May 21, 2017. https://www.americanprogress.org/issues/women/reports/2017/05/21/432758/womens-leadership-gap/

Williams, Melissa J. "The Price Women Leaders Pay for Assertiveness—and How to Minimize It." *Wall Street Journal.* May 30, 2016. https://www.wsj.com/articles/the-price-women-leaders-pay-fo r-assertivenessand-how-to-minimize-it-1464660240

Chapter 5 References: Influence

"3 in 5 Employees Did Not Negotiate Salary." May 2, 2016. Glassdoor. https://www.glassdoor.com/blog/3-5-u-s-employees-negotiate -salary/

Bacon, Terry. *Elements of Influence: The Art of Getting Others to Follow Your Lead.* New York: AMACOM Books, 2011.

Edmondson, Amy C. "Framing for Learning: Lessons in Successful Technology Implementation." *California Management Review*, 2003; 45(2): 34-54.

Friedman, Megan. "Here's the Transcript of Oprah's Inspirational Golden Globes Speech." January 7, 2018. *Harper's Bazaar.* https://www.harpersbazaar.com/culture/film-tv/a14551183/oprah-winfrey-golden-globes-speech-transcript/

Liebbrant, Andreas, and John List. "Do Women Avoid Salary Negotiations? Evidence from a Large Scale Natural Field Experiment." 2014. Harvard Kennedy School Women and Public Policy Program. http://gap.hks.harvard.edu/do-women-avoid-salary-negotiations-evidenc e-large-scale-natural-field-experiment

Lowe, Peggy. "How One Hospital Entices Doctors to Work in Rural America." NPR. February 2, 2012. https://www.npr.org/sections/health-shots/2012/02/02/145860801/how-one-hospital-entices-doctors-to-work-in-rural-america

Chapter 6 References: Transformational Leadership

Achor, Shawn, Andrew Reece, Gabriella Rosen Kellerman, and Alexi Bobichaux. "9 Out of 10 People Are Willing to Earn Less Money to Do More-Meaningful Work." *Harvard Business Review*. November 6, 2018. https://hbr.org/2018/11/9-out-of-10-people-are -willing-to-earn-less-money-to-do-more-meaningful-work

Arteche, A., Chamorro-Premuzic, T., Furnham, A., & Crump, J. "The Relationship of Trait EI with Personality, IQ and Sex in a UK Sample of Employees." *International Journal of Selection and Assessment*, 2008; 16(4), 421-426.

Baldoni, John. "Few Executives are Self-Aware, But Women Have the Edge." Harvard Business Review. May 9, 2013. https://hbr. org/2013/05/few-executives-are-self-aware

Bright Horizons. "New Research Shows the 'Mental Load' is Real and Significantly Impacts Working Mothers Both at Home and Work." https://www.brighthorizons.com/about-us/press-releases/ mental-load-impact-working-mothers-study

Burns, James MacGregor. *Leadership*. New York: Harper Collins, 1982.

Cool, Lisa Collier. "Are Male and Female Brains Different?" WebMD. https://www.webmd.com/brain/features/ how-male-female-brains-differ#1

Gerzema, John, and Michael D'Antonio. The Athena Doctrine: How Women (and the Men Who Think Like Them) Will Rule the Future. New York: Jossey-Bass, 2013.

Meshkat, Maryam, and Reza Nejati. "Does Emotional Intelligence Depend on Gender? A Study on Undergraduate English Majors of Three Iranian Universities." *SAGE Open*; 2017: 1–8. https://journals. sagepub.com/doi/pdf/10.1177/2158244017725796

Wingenbach, Tanja et al. "Sex Differences in Facial Emotion Recognition Across Varying Expression Intensity Levels from

Videos." *PloS One; 2018, 13(1)*. **https://www.ncbi.nlm.nih.gov/pmc/articles/PMC5749848/**

Chapter 7 References: Power of Peers

Lean In. "Lean In Circles." 2018. https://leanin.org/circles

Sandberg, Sheryl. *Lean In: Women, Work and the Will to Lead*. New York: Alfred A. Knopf, 2013.

Shapiro, Leon, and Leo Bottary. *The Power of Peers: How the Company You Keep Drives Leadership, Growth and Success*. New York: Routledge, 2016.

Uzzi, Brian. Research: Men and Women Need Different Networks to Succeed. *Harvard Business Review*, February 25, 2019.

About the
Author

D r. Mary Key is a master executive coach and facilitator, trusted advisor, author and speaker. She heads Key Associates, an organizational transformation consulting firm, and has an outstanding track record of helping leaders and organizations grow and thrive. She and her team have worked with Fortune 500 companies, Inc. 500 winners, and various entrepreneurial enterprises, government agencies and not-for-profit organizations. She has also consulted in Europe, Asia and Latin America.

Key has taken her over 25 years of experience coaching leaders and facilitating CEO and key leader peer groups and designed a unique peer forum experience for executive women. The purpose of the Key Women's Leadership Forum is to bring together women in leadership roles and focus on the whole self – mind, body, spirit and career. Founded in 2014, the women's forums address pressing issues, leveraging leadership influence and aligning your career with what is purposeful personally and professionally.

Key delivers keynotes and workshops for various clients and universities including Stanford University's Healthcare Leadership Development program. She addresses organizations that have developed programs for women in leadership such as Raymond James, Women in Baseball, Gerdau and others.

Before starting her own firm, Key worked in leadership roles at DDI (Development Dimensions International) and served as Vice President in a training and development company that was acquired by Learning International. After starting Key Associates, she was selected to be part of a national team that built Inc. Magazine's Eagles CEO program, in which CEOs of fast-growing companies came together to focus on each other's strategic business issues, achieving remarkable results.

Key is the author of several books including *CEO Road Rules: Right Focus, Right People, Right Execution* and *The Entrepreneurial Cat: 13 Ways to Transform Your Work Life*. She received her Ph.D. from the University of Virginia and her BS from the University of Massachusetts. She was selected to be part of the Society of International Business Fellows (SIBF), Leadership Florida, Athena Society, Association of Corporate Executive Coaches (ACEC) and the CEO Council.

Key lives in Tampa Bay with her husband Lewis and their three cats, Santini, Sophia and Princess.